Who Is Able?

THE DANA LOUISE CRYER STORY

WRITTEN BY
KIMBERLY ANN HOBBS
MICHAEL AND JULIE T. JENKINS

World Publishing and Productions

Who Is Able? The Dana Louise Cryer Story
Copyright © 2024 World Publishing and Productions

Published by World Publishing and Productions
PO Box 8722, Jupiter, FL 33468
Worldpublishingandproductions.com

All rights reserved. This book is protected under the copyright laws of the United States of America. No portion of this book may be reproduced, distributed, or transmitted in any form, including photocopying, recording, or other electronic or mechanical methods, without the written permission of the publisher, excepted in the case of brief quotations embodied in reviews and certain other non-commercial uses permitted by copyright law.

ISBN: 978-1-957111-37-7
Library of Congress Control Number: 2024945598

Scripture quotations marked KJV are taken from the King James Version. Public Domain.

Scripture quotations marked NIV are taken from THE HOLY BIBLE, NEW INTERNATIONAL VERSION®, NIV® Copyright © 1973, 1978, 1984, 2011 by Biblica, Inc.® Used by permission. All rights reserved worldwide.

Scripture quotations marked NIRV are taken from the Holy Bible, NEW INTERNATIONAL READER'S VERSION®. Copyright © 1995, 1996, 1998, 2014 by Biblica, Inc.®. All rights reserved worldwide. Used by permission.

Scripture quotations marked NLV are taken from the New Life Version, copyright © 1969 and 2003. Used by permission of Barbour Publishing, Inc., Uhrichsville, Ohio 44683. All rights reserved.

Foreword

You are about to read the extraordinary story of Dana Louise Cryer's life.

Who Is Able? The Dana Louise Cryer Story was birthed when Kimberly Hobbs asked a ministry partner, "Who do you know that I need to know?"

Her answer was, "Dana Louise Cryer has a story that will forever change you."

When Kimberly and Dana met, they both recognized it as a divine appointment arranged by God. As they got to know each other, it became clear that God had a purpose for this appointment—He wanted Dana's story to be written for the whole world to read.

It was not a new calling for Dana to share all God had done in her life. As you will read, she had been speaking to congregations and crowds for decades. But God was now asking her to take it another step. Before embarking on this project, our entire World Publishing and Productions staff prayed together with Dana, her family, and our sister ministry, Women World Leaders, seeking God's guidance and direction. Then, covered by the Holy Spirit, we began the journey of writing this remarkable story.

Dana's memory of these events is miraculously clear. We have endeavored to convey her story truthfully—praying that the Holy Spirit, who was there every step of the way, would use His power to guide us and keep us on track. And we know He did.

Several years ago, Dana told her story to a group of inmates, which is the backdrop for this book. Jocinda's character is a fictionalized account of an actual inmate Dana connected with and spoke to. We don't know that inmate's name or story, but we know God does, and He is holding her in His care. Our purpose in writing Jocinda's story is to draw awareness to how two people can be similarly mistreated and end up on different paths. But when we give God our pain and heartbreak, He radically protects, renews, and ushers in His glory through His forgiveness and grace.

We have prayed for you, dear reader. May God bless you through this story.

In Him,
Dana Louise Cryer
Kimberly Ann Hobbs
Michael & Julie T. Jenkins

Who Am I, Really?

I walked through the solid metal door, hearing it slam shut behind me with a clang that reverberated down the dark hallway. As I was led to my destination, gates continually locked behind me, one after another, with regularity, sealing off my freedom in a way that sent me reeling into my past as other sounds that continually looped in my sub-conscience again forced their way to the surface of my mind...

The car coming down the road with its tires crunching against the gravel.

The tormenting tapping—waking me from my restless sleep.

The distant whistle and rhythm of the train—which grew to be my source of comfort.

And the sound of those words that forever changed my life: "Shut up."

Glancing down in discomfort at the fancy clothes and the shine of glitzy jewelry I had unwillingly adorned myself with, following the orders of the correction officer, I thought, *This is not me. This is not who I am.* Wondering again, *Why did I have to dress like this. Is all this necessary to share my testimony?*

Continuing to walk down the hallway, I approached the area where I would speak and share the story of my life.

Ahead of me, in the crowded room of women, the correctional officer approached and instructed me where to stand. She was a woman who commanded respect.

My senses were overwhelmed with the thick smell of so many bodies congregating in one room. The hollow sound of captivity and the voices of the guards barking orders echoed in my ears even as I was still aware of the bars clanging in the distance. My vision was filled with vulgar gestures and slouching bodies. As slanderous words rose from the crowd, mocking me, insecurities from my past bubbled up inside.

Approaching the microphone, dressed as an imposter, my misgivings were validated by the steely and snarling faces looking back at me. Every size, shape, color, and age group. All dressed in orange. All glaring with disgust at who they perceived me to be. I even heard the words, "She thinks she's all that."

Off to the side, the correctional officer gained control of the nasty chaos. My jitters began to subside as I sought to understand that the vile ugliness spewing out of the inmates was only coming from a place of hurt and pain. Only God knew all the personal, heart-wrenching stories hidden in that room. But here I was—called by God to tell my own personal, heart-wrenching story. A story that, in the end, brought me more joy than the human spirit could ever fully comprehend.

The correctional officer began to address the galley of women. I was blown away by her preconceived plan.

"Residents, you're probably thinking that this person standing next to me is a highly successful, educated, accomplished citizen. That she grew up in a privileged household." She accented the word "privileged," annunciating three distinct syllables. "She sure looks like she went to fine schools. Earned her degrees. And spends much of her time shopping at high-end stores."

The snarling faces became more agitated.

"I mean, just look at her. She's got it all together. Easy life. No baggage."

They harshly sneered; many stomped their feet in protest of my very presence.

My eyes fixed on a woman in the second row as she slouched deeper in her chair. Jocinda, I would later learn her name, murmured, loud enough for me to hear, "Yeah. She sure is all that," drawing out the word "all" as if it encompassed everything that ever was and ever would be.

"Well, you're wrong. You're all wrong."

The room suddenly grew quieter.

"This woman grew up in hell. She didn't have a family. She didn't have food to eat. Heck, she didn't even go to school."

My face grew hot as I stood as if on display.

"She was a teenager who didn't know how to read or write. Or barely even speak. She had no clothes."

I remembered the shame.

"She had no one who loved her. She didn't even know what love was."

That was true. It was all true.

"She never had a father or mother," she enunciated.

I felt like I had been punched as the words hung in the air.

The correctional officer paused as she peered into the faces of the women before her. "Well, looks don't always tell the whole story," she continued pointedly. "But I'm sure none of you have ever been misjudged."

I noticed the inmates begin to sit up straighter, and the sounds in the room muffled to a silence as their glares began to soften.

Faces full of question marks populated the atmosphere as the suddenly alert listeners showed signs of wanting to hear more.

After a moment, she continued, "Welcome, Dana Louise Cryer. Dana, will you share your story?"

I took a sharp breath. Silence swallowed the room. And I began to reveal the pain and suffering I had endured. The pain that ultimately led me to a life of unimaginable joy.

In the Beginning

Hello, ladies. Thank you for having me.

As we begin our time together, I'd like to take you back to my earliest memories—they are happy ones. When I was five years old, I lived with my Aunt Mildred and Uncle Howard in the mountains of Flagstaff, Arizona. As I think about those carefree days in the cozy cabin, specific scenes loop in my mind.

Aunt Mildred and Uncle Howard always included me in everything. Even our daily chores were joyful. Uncle Howard and I would make a celebration out of creating small stacks with the wood that we used to fuel the big black stove in the kitchen. And because I was so short, he made a small bench for me to stand on so I could help Aunt Mildred put the sticks of wood into the hole on the stove. They spoiled me with so much attention.

Aunt Mildred cooked the most delicious dinners—they are still ingrained in my mind, tucked away forever. The aroma of stews, soups, beans, and cornbread always filled the cabin, but the taste of it was always even better than the smell. My mouth still waters thinking about those foods today.

Some of my favorite times with Aunt Mildred were when we baked together. Although we didn't have much, we always had dessert after every meal. I loved preparing the cookie dough and pulling the hot pans full of tasty treats out of the oven. That sweet, delightful smell of cinnamon and sugar cookies brought happiness to my heart.

Eating dinner and dessert was also a special time. We would sit around the table for hours, laughing as we shared our daily escapades.

Then, after dinner, was bathtime. Aunt Mildred would clean my little body in the hot bath, replacing the toils of the day with smells of lavender and rose from her handmade soap. She instructed me to raise my hands high as she slipped my clean pj's over my head. I remember looking at her face, her beautiful smile shining down at me as my head popped out of the hole in my pajamas. We would always laugh about it. Then Aunt Mildred would brush my long hair with her gentle hands, smoothing out every knot and tangle.

A big walk-in fireplace in the family room provided warmth and comfort—both physically and emotionally. After my bath, we would join Uncle Howard on the sofa as Aunt Mildred played her accordion and we all sang together. Melodious sounds filled the room with happiness. When I got sleepy, one of them would tuck me into my clean, warm bed, where I would stay safe and secure until the smell of cooking bacon woke me in the morning.

During the day, I often went outside to play, dressed with care by my aunt. The joy that filled her soul as she watched me romp and play was apparent. Unbeknownst to me at the time, I was an answer to their cries of barrenness. I didn't know it at the time, but when I was just two days old, I was sold for $1 to Uncle Howard and Aunt Mildred by my daddy, Uncle Howard's brother.

One ordinary day, I ran outside wearing my Mary Janes, the special shoes I treasured. I hurried to the swing Uncle Howard had made me out of an old tire and a rope he found in the barn. The smell of stew wafted from the window as I swung on the tire without a care in the world. We didn't have much, but together, the three of us had a happy home. Little did I know those happy days would soon be nothing more than a memory.

Jocinda

Jocinda slouched in her chair, listening in disbelief. She had only come to break up the monotony of her day.

Please. Did the warden just say this woman with the fancy clothes grew up in hell? Hell? I guess the warden didn't know her story after all. Now, I have to sit here and listen to this white woman who lived in the mountains eating fresh cookies and bathing in lavender whine about how rough she had it?

Jocinda rolled her eyes.

She has no idea what hell is.

Hell is not having a future. Hell is knowing that every day will be the same and the best you can do is survive. Hell is realizing that this place, with its concrete walls, cell doors, barbed wire fences, and guards who don't care if you live or die, is still better than where you came from.

That's what hell is.

Jocinda sat back and listened.

At least listening to this white woman with her nice shoes is something different from the monotony of the everyday life of a black woman serving time in prison.

Oh, this lady's story is different than anything I've ever lived. My life and her life couldn't be more different.

Taken

The sun was shining, and the sky was bright blue the unforgettable day my world changed. Uncle Howard was doing his chores out back as Aunt Mildred worked inside. They had ushered me out front to play, and I was having a great time, enjoying being alone as I flew freely through the air on the tire swing that hung from the large tree, my hair blowing in the breeze behind me.

Suddenly, the sound of singing birds was interrupted by the crunching noise of an old vehicle approaching. Nobody ever came down our road, and I loved seeing people. I put my foot down to stop the swing, knocking the shoe off my foot. As it landed in the dirt, I looked up and saw an old yellow station wagon stop in front of our yard.

A man got out of the car and began talking to me. I don't remember what he said as I innocently walked toward him.

I often wonder why I got into his car. I know he instructed me to, and I listened. Maybe I was just used to being obedient. Maybe I thought I knew him. Or maybe he forced me. There is a block in my memory. It would be the first block of many.

What I do remember is being frightened by the definitive slamming of the car door. I sat in the front seat, running my fingers along the cracks in the worn-out upholstery. I was too small to see out the window, but I wanted to. I wondered, *Where are Uncle Howard and Aunt Mildred?*

As the stranger slid in beside me, I fixed my eyes on the steering wheel, noticing his dirty hands with split fingernails.

We began to speed away from all that was familiar to me. Then I saw a gun that he had placed on the seat between us, and I became more afraid. I started crying and told the man I wanted to go back home. He instructed me to "Shut up."

Those two words would shape my childhood with fear for years to come.

I grasped the door handle, trying not to be thrown around by the movement of the car as we careened down the winding roads. Through the haze on the old car window, I could see the tops of green pine trees whisk by. Being jostled around, the smell of gasoline and warm, stagnant air made my stomach queasy. I knew we were going far from my home.

The ride seemed like an eternity to the five-year-old child who knew no world apart from the shelter of Uncle Howard and Aunt Mildred's cozy house.

When the clunking of the car finally stopped, the man got out. Thinking we had returned to my home, I breathed a sigh of relief and reached for the door, ready to run and melt into the comforting arms of Uncle Howard. But instead, the tall, angry stranger suddenly yanked my door open and reached for my arm. He pulled me out of the car, and my heart sank as I realized I was not home.

His dirty fingernails dug into the skin on my arm. Even though the wind now hit my face, the breeze couldn't take away the vile smell that seemed to emanate from his rotting soul. Stumbling over my feet, unable to keep my footing, my one remaining beautiful shoe got scuffed and beaten by the dirt and rocks he was dragging me across, breaking the buckle.

Getting frustrated, he picked me up and threw me under his arm. My stomach was shoved into his side, making my whole body jolt and causing me to lose my shoe. The intensity of fear that gripped me at that moment forced everything from my insides out. Chunks of cornbread projected out of my mouth all over his legs. Although my tears continued to flow, I obediently kept silent for fear of being hurt more.

He threw me down in the dirt and yelled at me to stop crying. I fell on my knees, and they began to bleed. Paralyzed with fear, I looked up and realized that the only thing in sight was a small, dreary shack. Its dilapidated four walls held up a rusty, metal roof that looked like it hadn't been entered in years. He opened the door, turned back toward me, and forcefully dragged me inside.

A mildewed, musty smell hit me like a physical punch. The jagged edges of darkened wood from the floor pierced my skin as I fell once more.

The door slammed shut with an echo that haunted me for days, months, and years. He pushed me down onto a dirty mattress lying on the floor. Not being able to help myself, I cried so hard as he climbed on top of me and held me down, putting the gun next to my head and telling me once again to shut up.

All I can remember next is the excruciating pain that would not stop as he forcefully ripped at my clothes and pushed himself between my legs. I could not move.

The fear almost silenced me, but it hurt so bad I couldn't hold in my screams.

His toxic breath infected me like a disease, even as I felt the shearing pain of his hard flesh mutilating my five-year-old vagina. Then he flipped me over. My face crushed into the rankness of the putrid mattress as the pain intensified beyond comprehension. I couldn't understand what was happening as he shoved his flesh into me once again from behind.

Little did I know that the brutality of all he was doing to me and the pain that was tearing me apart was only the beginning.

Jocinda

Jocinda listened.

Her cellmate, Vivi, who was serving ten years for being a repeat offender and trafficking drugs, leaned over and said, "Can you believe this? There is no way this can be real. No one would do that to a little kid."

But Jocinda knew all too well that it was real and could surely happen. It had happened to her.

Immediately, she understood what the white woman with the nice shoes had been through. Jocinda had felt it all, too. Her mind went back to her own childhood.

I remember the night when my daddy, if you could even call him that, beat mama so badly in a drug-fueled rage that she almost died. I was five years old—the same age the lady on the stage had been—when, for the first time, I realized that life would not be easy.

I saw the fear in mama's eyes when daddy repeatedly kicked the tar out of the only woman who had ever protected me.

I couldn't fully understand what was happening, but I knew it was bad. In a final fit of rage, daddy spit on mama and then walked out. I saw her crawl to the bedroom, sobbing, and then I fell asleep on the floor, trying to block the scene from my mind. That was the last time I saw mama. Later, I figured she left to escape the drugs, the constant abuse and neglect, and, of course, the beatings. But she had also left me and little Violet to live in our own version of hell.

I could never understand why mama didn't take us with her. Anywhere would have been better than where we were. And I never forgave her. When I woke up on that hard floor, there was nothing but silence around me. I knew that Violet and I were on our own with that monster we called daddy. And I knew I had to protect Violet at all costs.

Waking Up

As the morning light began to fill the darkness, I woke up crying for Aunt Mildred, anxious for her to come rescue me from my nightmare. But all the pain that permeated my little body was real. Very real. My crying continued until I realized my aunt wasn't coming. Nobody was coming.

My tummy was rumbling with hunger, but there were no good smells of Aunt Mildred's breakfast.

I reached for Sarah, my baby doll, but she was nowhere to be found. Neither was my soft, cuddly blanket that always wrapped me securely at night. Instead, I saw unfamiliar and scary surroundings.

High on the wall above me was a small, filthy, cracked window. Looking through it from below, I could see green leaves that surely were attached to a tree. I imagined it was similar to the big tree from which Uncle Howard hung my tire swing. The thought of my beloved swing as I remembered the last familiar thing I had seen made me cry. When would I see it again?

The dreary room was lit only by the pale light that filtered in through that one window. Through my tears, I strained to take in my surroundings.

Besides the mattress on the floor, there was a garbage can and a bucket in one corner, looming in the shadows. And there was some sort of counter along one wall. That was about it. Realizing I was completely alone in the quiet, my fear intensified, and I began to shake uncontrollably.

The dirty, shredded mattress was so thin that my bottom felt like it was directly on the floor. It was sticky and damp, making me want to get off it. But trying to move caused wrenching pain. I wanted to scream but didn't dare, remembering the order he had yelled over and over: "Shut up." The words echoing in my mind made me freeze in fear.

I wondered where he was and what he would do to me next. I was afraid to move or make any noise at all. I hoped my stillness would keep me invisible.

Jocinda

I tried to be invisible too, Jocinda thought. *I figured if I were invisible, daddy wouldn't hurt me. But it didn't turn out that way.*

I had no idea what my life was to become.

It started with daddy's friend, Frank. We were supposed to call him Uncle Frank. He came to our little house in Belmont. I was too young to know it then, but Belmont was one of the most dangerous areas of Detroit, and Uncle Frank fit right in. He and daddy smoked crack. I remember the sound it made when they inhaled on the pipe and I will never forget the smell—like burnt plastic.

Daddy said he needed it, and when he didn't have money for it, he got mean and desperate. That's where I came in.

I remember Uncle Frank giving daddy the bag with the small white rocks. Then daddy took me by the hand and pulled me hard to the couch where Uncle Frank was sitting. He told me I had to do what Uncle Frank told me, or I would get the belt. Daddy had hit me before with his belt, and I knew how much it hurt. I also remembered what he did to mama, so I knew I had to obey or he would kick me and spit on me, too.

Uncle Frank smelled like sweat. He was so fat, with folds of skin that were as black as night. He was much darker than me and Violet. He took my hand, and I followed him to the bedroom. There was a mattress on the floor. I KNOW what a mattress on the floor means. Sometimes daddy's friends would sleep there, though I don't know how they could, as bad as it smelled.

Uncle Frank pushed me down and started to unbuckle his pants. I thought he was gonna hit me with his belt, like daddy had done, and I started to cry. I didn't know what I had done wrong to make me get a whipping. But he didn't whip me. What he did was so much worse.

He lay on top of me and spread my legs. I had no idea what was happening. Then I felt him. The pain felt like it was going to split me in two. I screamed, but he didn't stop. I remember trying to understand what was happening. Why was he doing this? What had I done that he would hurt me this way?

He was done quickly. I remember him smiling as he got off me.

I will never forget that face. I whimpered and cried quietly so no one would hear. I pushed my face into the mattress and tried to wish away the pain.

Yeah...it's real. Lots of people treat kids that way.

He's Back

As I lay silently, I heard the sound of tires on the dusty road outside. I sat up, not knowing where to hide. I quickly slid off the mattress and pushed myself under it. As I did, splinters of wood pierced my skin, but I didn't dare make a sound. He was back.

I shook silently as the door crashed open. He reached under the mattress and grabbed my arm, pulling me across the splintered wood floor. My dress ripped as my body was drug and thrown back onto the mattress. He screamed at me to shut up. All I could do was whimper in fear.

He threw the gun down with a heavy clunk next to my head, a silent threat reminding me not to resist. He unbuckled his pants, and I felt the hair on his skinny legs as he smothered my body with his. Then, the same pain that had ripped through me the first time now returned, reopening my wounds, while the smell of his breath engulfed my whole head and made me vomit in my mouth.

When he was done, I lay there, a sweaty, stinky mess. He stammered to get up as slurred words came out of his mouth that I couldn't understand. Then, aiming for the bucket in the corner, he urinated all over the floor. Stumbling across the dimly lit room, he propped himself up on the wood casing that I was not tall enough to see the top of. I heard the sound of running water coming from a faucet and saw him cup his hands and take a drink.

Is he going to offer me some water? I am so thirsty.

But he didn't.

He stood upright and headed for the door.

Is he going to take me with him or leave me here alone again, without food and water? Do I even want to go with him?

With his hand on the door, he yelled at me again, scaring me even more. He told me never to open the door because big, hungry bears surrounded the shack, and they were waiting to eat me if I tried to get out.

The door slammed shut.

After the wheels of the car rolled down the path, all that was left was silence.

I looked up at what I now knew was a sink, knowing I was too small to reach it. My body was hurting so badly, and the mattress had gotten bloodier from my wounds. Blood was everywhere. My legs were covered with blood. I wondered if I was going to die. But all that didn't matter because I was so thirsty.

I mustered my strength and hobbled to the counter. Despite the pain screaming from every inch of me, I had to figure out a way to get to the water.

I grasped the counter with my hands and tried to climb, but there was nothing to hold onto. I slumped to the ground in tears, not knowing what to do. I just knew I would never be able to get a drink.

As I lay on the ground and sobbed, memories of cooking in the kitchen with Aunt Mildred flooded my mind. I could almost smell the fresh bread baking as I remembered standing on my stool, reaching my little hands across the counter to help prepare the soup. I thought of the many times Aunt Mildred reminded me to wash my hands and how, if I stood on my tiptoes on the stool, I could just reach the faucet.

Suddenly, my eyes sprung open.

When I opened them, they went directly to the old bucket. It was as if something inside me was telling me that if I turned the bucket upside down, I could climb on it to reach the water—just like I had used the stool Uncle Howard had made for me back home.

Carefully stepping around his urine on the floor, I grabbed the bucket and, placing it near the counter, turned it upside down and lifted my knee to hoist myself up on it. The surface was hard and scratchy, but I was so thirsty that I barely noticed. I carefully steadied myself, sliding from my knee to my foot and balancing myself on the overturned bucket as I stood up.

The room looked different now. Above the mattress, I could now see the trunk of a tree through the window. But more importantly, the faucet was now in my sight. Despite wanting water so badly, I still couldn't reach it. As I lurched out, a single drop of water fell from the spigot onto my wrist. I quickly jerked back to put my wrist to my mouth so I wouldn't lose that single drop. Just then, the bucket wobbled, causing me to lose my balance and fall to the floor. In exhaustion and pain, I began crying again.

I just wanted someone to take care of me.

But I was alone.

Somehow, I knew that I needed water to survive. So, I chose to be as strong as I could. I raised myself up again and started over.

Place the bucket. This time, closer to the counter.

Climb up. Ignore the hard and scratchy surface.

Slide my feet under me. And...slowly, now...stand.

Okay. I made it this far.

This time, I apprehensively raised to my tiptoes, being careful, just like Aunt Mildred had taught me back in the kitchen. I cautiously leaned against the counter, balancing my little body, being sure not to tip the bucket and fall. I stretched my arms till they were burning and felt the smooth, cold metal of the faucet knob turn beneath my hand. I used my free hand, as the other hand still gripped the counter for balance, and finally splashed the refreshing water into my dry, cracked mouth.

Mesmerized by the sweet taste, I lost myself as I stared at the stream of water before me. I thought about helping Aunt Mildred wash the dishes after dinner in the sudsy, warm water, my belly full of dinner and delicious dessert.

Then I began crying again.

I longed to be home in my own kitchen, with its familiar smells and sounds.

Jocinda

The woman with the nice shoes wanted to be home. At least she had a home. I never had a home.

I only ever had a place to live—no warm baths, no mother to love me, not even any food. Except for the free food we got at school and whatever daddy and his friends left behind after they passed out.

Daddy took all the money to buy drugs. When he did eat, I would muster all my nerve to ask if there was something for Violet and me. Most of the time, he just laughed. If he had pizza, we might get a slice to share between us. Violet was a year younger than me; I knew I had to protect her. I was the only person she could count on, so I always gave her the bigger part of the pizza slice.

I often dug through the pantry or refrigerator, hoping to find anything we could eat. It was like being a beggar in my own home.

I remember the day I thought about the trash.

I went outside and found the neighbor's can next to their garage. It was like I had found a treasure. There was much more food in that trash can than was ever in our house. I grabbed as much as I could with my little hands and carried it back inside. That was the first time I ever remember not being hungry. Violet and I ate what other people didn't want. Later, I would laugh because we were the children that nobody wanted.

We were trash eating trash.

Daddy came home that night and found the chicken bones we had sucked clean. He asked me where they came from, and when I told him, he slapped me hard across the face. The blood from my split lip was warm; my mouth immediately started to swell. He screamed that we were never to do that again or he would kill us both.

He glared at me and said if I didn't straighten up, he would choke Violet and make me watch.

I believed him.

I would have to find another way to get food.

I had to protect Violet.

Hunger Sets In

Uncle Howard and I used to stand on the back porch at dusk and watch the sun go down. We would tell each other about the best part of our day and the fun we had planned for the morning. But now the shack got dark again and again, and there was nobody to share memories with and nothing to look forward to. Because nobody was coming for me. I was alone.

The days came and went, and I got hungrier and hungrier. The space under the counter, where it seemed like food should be if there ever was food, was empty, except for spider webs and rusty nails. I even emptied the trash piece by piece, hoping to find something. All I found were empty brown bottles that smelled like his breath and some crumpled-up paper. There was not even a crumb of food.

There was nothing else in the cabin to even search through, and I didn't dare open the door for fear of the bears. My stomach hurt so bad—like it had never hurt before. I felt like I wanted to throw up, but there was nothing in me to throw up. And I grew weak; it was so hard to move, which didn't matter much because there was nowhere to go. During those first days, I had used the corner for a toilet, but now, I didn't even need to go to the bathroom. I spent day after day laying on the mattress, wondering when I would eat again.

I don't know how long I had been lying there staring at the door when a familiar but unwelcome sound broke the silence. It was a car in the distance, the foreboding sound of tires crunching the gravel. I was so scared I could barely breathe. My thoughts of hunger dissipated as a greater fear enveloped me.

I crawled to the corner of the room to try to hide in the shadows, remembering the excruciating pain the stranger inflicted. The agony that I had tried so hard to block out returned in full force, making me shake in fear as I anticipated him doing those terrible things to me again. The car got closer. Then it stopped. Almost instantaneously, the door opened, and he was back.

He flung a paper bag onto the cabinet with a thud as I cowered in the shadows. There were no words spoken, only the gruffness of his actions as he grabbed me and threw me back on the mattress. Again, placing the gun by my head. The brutal force of his actions and the smell of him repulsed me, but it was nothing compared to the pain that ripped through my body.

Looking back, it is clear that the smell that emanated from his pores was that of alcohol and smoke. His bony body indicated that he himself seldom ate, yet to my tiny person, his strength was overpowering. I still didn't know who he was or why he chose to steal and abuse me, but I knew I hated everything about him.

It wasn't until much later that I would realize who he was and who was able to save me from the repercussions of this horrific situation.

After what seemed like an eternity of lying beneath his heaviness, the snoring stopped as he woke up. Groggily, he reached for his gun and pulled himself off me. He staggered to the door, slamming it behind him as he left. After the car rolled away, the only sound left was my sobs. I hadn't imagined that I could ever hurt worse than I did the first time, but I couldn't escape the pain that now shackled me from head to toe.

Night came. I still didn't move. My hunger pains screamed even louder than before.

As the morning light came through the window, I noticed the bag he threw on the counter was still there. I pulled up my aching body. With each movement, his smell was released from my tattered dress, where his body excretions were ingrained, making me want to vomit again. Almost in a trance, I made my way to the counter and climbed up on the overturned bucket. Grasping for the bag, I felt the weight inside. My eyes widened as I looked inside and saw some loose crackers and an almost empty jar of peanut butter.

That was how I lived.

Alone and hungry.

Dreading the sound of the car and his foreboding entrance, which always brought vile pain but sometimes gave me a chance to eat. When he left food meant for me, it was usually peanut butter and crackers. Sometimes, he threw a half-eaten sandwich in the trash, which I fished out after he was gone.

At first, I gobbled the food as soon as I could lay my hands on it. Then I learned to ration it, knowing it could be days or weeks before he would return. I was always afraid of him returning, yet I longed for the paper bag of food.

The shack became my new existence.

The night sounds continued to frighten me. I had once enjoyed going outside, but it had become a scary place in my new life as the thought of bears waiting to devour me outside the door always lurked in my mind. The weather turned, and the leaves fell outside the dingy window. And then came the cold. It was a misery I had yet to experience.

Not having been given blankets or even more clothes, I covered myself with the crumpled paper bags of trash and slid under the mattress for warmth. Even then, I shivered at night, longing for the sun to peek through the filthy window, bringing me some sense of warmth.

Eventually, the seasons changed, the leaves started to grow outside my window, and the nights weren't so cold. Then, the summertime heat intensified, causing me to sweat and long for the fresh breeze.

Throughout the change of seasons, my fear never left.

And the pain of his abuse was regularly renewed as he sliced himself through my body time and again.

Jocinda

J ocinda listened to the woman and knew exactly what the sounds in the night that frightened her were like.

I had heard them, too. It always started with laughter. How crazy is it that the worst part of my life always started with laughter?

Daddy would have a friend or some friends over. They would sit in the room with the couch and do drugs. Eventually, he would call to me and make me stand there while he stroked my hair like he was proud of me, but I knew he was just showing me off like someone would pet a dog they were about to sell.

One time, I tried to hide when his friends came over. He called for me, and I didn't come. I crawled under the bed and played dead. I tried not to breathe as he stomped through our little house, screaming my name. He came into the room, and I remember thinking that I wished there was somebody who was able to make this all go away.

Daddy found me under the bed. He reached under and grabbed my hair. He pulled me out from under the bed and called me a little bitch for making him look for me. He slapped me hard. I remember thinking I was going to pass out. Then he threw me on the bed. I tried to get away, but he slapped me again.

Then he called out to his friends. "This here little lady is ready."

He reached down, grabbed my pants, and ripped them off. I knew the pain was coming again. In walked a tall man in a white T-shirt. He had bad teeth and smelled like smoke. He got on top of me as daddy left the room.

I closed my eyes and waited for it to be over.

A Connection

Standing before the inmates, I paused before I resumed my story.

I took in the sets of now-softening eyes looking back at me from the prison floor, again noticing Jocinda in the second row, still sitting staunchly. But now, a tear rolled down her cheek.

I remarked how incredible it still is to me that I learned to live entirely on my own at such a young age. I told the residents, who were now listening intently, that no matter what we go through in life, we are always taken care of in ways that may seem unexplainable.

"I'm guessing some of you can relate to being abandoned and alone."

My eyes met Jocinda's. It was like we shared the same pain. There was an unimaginable depth of despair, but somehow, hidden in the look between us, there was a sense of hope. Maybe it was just a glimmer, but I was sure it was there.

My story was painful. But I forged ahead.

Learning to Exist

As the years passed, the daily life I had lived with my aunt and uncle began to fade from my memory. I could no longer recall faces, voices, or even words. And without a reason to speak, my own voice seemed to disappear.

The sounds outside the shack were my constant companions. To occupy the endless hours, I would often sit on the mattress, my back propped against the wall under the window, listening. In the beginning, many noises frightened me. But the longer I listened, the more my senses grew attuned to hearing all the rhythms around me, which became familiar and almost comforting.

The breeze in the trees became my lullaby. The cheery song of the birds added brightness to the dreariness. And the rain, when it would fall gently, was sweet and playful. By far, my favorite sound was the train whistle in the distance. I would sit and wait for hours, wondering when I would next hear its soothing sound.

But there were also the awful sounds that would haunt me for years to come.

Sometimes, I thought I heard the menacing growls of the bears outside waiting to eat me; that was enough to keep me hidden away.

And the gentle rain could quickly change to terror when the treacherous winds blew and thunderous booms from the lightning strikes pierced my ears. At times, it felt like the shack, the only shelter protecting me from the outside, might be destroyed. During those storms, I would hide under the mattress to try to silence the deafening roars of nature and the even more debilitating thoughts in my head that made me wonder what would happen to me should my protection be blown away.

But what I thought of as my protection, the flimsy walls of the shack, in reality, did nothing to shield me when I heard the most horrific sound of all: the car tires crunching the gravel as the man returned. Bringing more pain.

Jocinda

Jocinda thought about the bears. She had her own bears.

As this lady told her story, it seemed like it was becoming more and more like the dark path she and Violet had walked. The same path that led her here, to this prison. From one place of no escape to another.

I lost track of how many men daddy gave me to. Those were my "bears." But they were not outside. They were brought in by the one person who should have been protecting me. But he loved his drugs more than he ever loved me and Violet. The smoking and needles brought him happiness and escape from the miserable life he had made for himself. Me and Violet? We were just goods to be sold so he could stay drugged up. I hated him for so many things, but I hated him most for that.

Daddy would occasionally bring home clothes for me and Violet as we grew. They were never much more than hand-me-down rags, but I was thankful to get them. When it was time for us to go to school, daddy told me that if Violet or I ever told anyone what happened at our house, he would hurt Violet really bad and make me watch. I knew he would kill us. We were nothing to him.

When I was 8 or 9, I can't remember exactly, I made the decision to leave the house to find some food. No matter how mad daddy got, I had to provide for Violet. No one else would. I distinctly remember trying to clean my dress so I could slip out and not be thought of as a beggar. I didn't want to draw any unnecessary attention to myself. I thought if I could just make it down to the gas station two blocks away, I could get us something to eat.

It was Thanksgiving day. With school on break, we hadn't had any food in days. My plan was to wait for daddy to pass out and then slip out. Once I got to the gas station, I would have to steal whatever food I could find there, because I had no money. We were both so hungry. I had to take care of things myself. I had seen the images of the kids in Africa on the TV and how the lady said they were starving. For only 25 cents per day, you could save a child. I wondered if Violet and I were going to look like that. No one was going to give us 25 cents a day.

Daddy passed out around 2:30 during the Lions' football game. I knew it was my chance. I told Violet to be very quiet and stay in our bedroom. I silently opened the back door and slipped outside. I took a deep breath as I felt the cool breeze hit me. I walked quickly out to the sidewalk and started for the gas station. There were very few people out, which was good. None of daddy's friends would see me, and for that, I was very thankful.

I was almost there when I heard someone call my name. My heart sank. It was Frank. Uncle Frank. Daddy's friend who had hurt me many times over the years. "Does your daddy know you are out here, girl? If he finds out, he ain't gonna be too happy, is he?"

I remember I thought about lying, but nothing came to mind. All I could say was, "Yes, sir. He would be mad."

Uncle Frank smiled and said this could be our little secret, but I would have to repay him. I didn't know exactly what that meant, but it was certainly not a good thing.

Yeah. I had my own bears.

Years Pass

It was difficult to track the passage of time, but my tattered dress became shorter and shorter, becoming more like a rag that hung on me as the threads wore through. I could now see out the window without standing on my tiptoes, and getting to the faucet was a simpler task.

There were gaps in the walls of the cabin; I would get on my hands and knees and peak through them. Until one time, I was met with the beady eyes of a rat. I flew back onto the mattress, vowing never to look through the crack again.

The pain inflicted regularly on my body and the hunger, which never left me, began to shape my thoughts about myself. Adding to my shame, the smell of my own body began to nauseate me. I longed for a bath and new clothes. His reactions to my stench verified that I was not imagining things. But being called a pig, and worse, destroyed any sense of self-confidence that I had remaining. Unable to express my needs and ask for soap or a dress that fit, I was continually silenced and threatened with the words, "I will kill you if you talk."

Despite the constant pain and fear, each time he left, I experienced a sense of relief. I would return to my comfort place, listening for the sounds.

One day, while sitting on the mattress with my back against the wall, a sound seemed to come from out of the past. It was faint, and I struggled to hear it more clearly. Putting my ear against the wall of the shack, I strained to listen as the sound grew louder. It was getting closer. Crawling on my hands and knees, I followed the faint sound as it moved toward the front of the shack. The meows made me know that there was something just inches away, on the other side of the wood planks, that could bring me love and joy and comfort. As it moved to the front of the shack, the only barrier to my comfort was the door.

And then the sound stopped.

Do I dare defy the man's fearful instructions never to go outside? Why did the sound stop? I wondered.

I caught my breath as the mewing began again.

Standing to my feet, I bravely placed my hand on the door latch. Then I paused, standing there for a moment, still listening to the whimpering, which had now intensified. Mustering my courage, I maneuvered the handle as grave fear washed over me.

Carefully, I cracked the door open, allowing a beam of bright light to come in that made me squint. As I pushed the door slowly, afraid of my own actions, I searched the ground, determined to find the source of the crying.

I so desperately wanted the comfort of a little animal that I didn't even notice the open sky beckoning me to freedom or that there were no bears in sight.

Then I saw it.

A soft, fluffy black furball was looking up at me. Its tiny mouth opened wide, releasing the whimsical whisper that had drawn me to the forbidden place.

What a sight!

I immediately forgot my fear and everything that held me captive inside the shack. Stepping outside, I reached down in the dirt and lifted the tiny life to my chest, holding it ever so tightly. Feeling an emotion from inside me that I remembered from my days with Uncle Howard and Aunt Mildred, I promised I would never let him go. I would always protect him.

I quickly retreated and shut the door, my heart beating fast but enthralled with the precious baby I held in my arms.

Gently tiptoeing to the mattress, I sat down, cuddling the kitty and stroking his fur over and over and over. I spent hours gently touching him and staring at the beauty of this little life, who was now sharing my surroundings. He settled in my arms and fell asleep as his purring became my new favorite sound. I knew I had to feed him and take care of him, but all I could do was get water from the sink and hold it in my hand for him to lick. Oh, the joy that the little lick brought to my hand! Its soft, gentle, wet touch tickled my hand, making me giggle. Another new sound I hadn't heard in a very long time was released from me. I wanted this moment with my new friend to never end.

We played together and cuddled until night came. When we lay down for bed, I hugged him tightly, never wanting to let go. The darkness, which surrounded me with loneliness every night, felt different. Despite it stealing my loving gaze and preventing me from seeing my petite companion, I was wrapped with joy by the kitty's presence. I soon fell into the soundest sleep I had experienced since being brought to the shack. With a smile ingrained on my face.

The beaming lights of morning woke me, coming in through the dirty window. I opened my eyes, thinking it was just another day alone. Suddenly, I remembered my new friend. *Where is he?* I turned from side to side in a panic, looking for him. He was nowhere near me. I sat up and looked around the room, still not seeing him anywhere.

Where is my friend?

Then, I realized the unthinkable.

The kitty was crushed underneath me. He was not moving. I tried and tried to get him to play with me, but he lay there limp. He was dead. I had suffocated him in my sleep.

My sadness overwhelmed me. I will never forget that moment of loss.

Jocinda

At least I wasn't alone.

I had Violet. She was my only friend. She understood. Thankfully, even though she was only a year younger than me, daddy never used her the way he used me. I had no idea why. I guess I will never know.

Violet was always much smaller than me. Even as a baby, she was so small. Maybe it was because mama didn't take care of herself when she was pregnant. She didn't have any of those vitamins or the right food or doctor visits. She just got pregnant and was supposed to deal with it. That's what she did. And Violet was small and sickly.

Once mama left us, I became Violet's mom. I made sure she had food even when I didn't have any. I always gave her the best of the clothes that daddy brought home. She slept with me. I would always put on the radio for her to listen to while I was "working," as daddy called it. I didn't want her to hear when I was in pain. That happened a lot.

I knew I had to take care of Violet as best I could. I taught her to talk and read and told her she had to be good in school. She was quiet, and that was good. We could never tell anyone what life at home was like, or daddy would hurt us. I knew what he would do to Violet. He was mean and had told me how he would hurt her and make me watch. I hated him. I didn't know how, but I would protect her no matter what.

I would never let daddy hurt Violet.

Growing Up

Time passed. My hair grew and grew. I spent hours combing through it with my fingers, remembering the feel of my kitty. I noticed hair growing on other parts of my body, too. The new smells that now came from my body sickened me.

My fingertips were often clumped with blood from chewing them. I was hungry and full of anxiety and fear. Biting my nails became a daily routine. I even sat on the mattress and contorted my body so I could bite my toenails so they wouldn't grow disgustingly long.

Maturing into an adolescent in the shack brought its own issues. I'll never forget the horror of waking up to find myself swimming in the blood that was all underneath my body. I had grown accustomed to bleeding, but this was different. The man hadn't been there, and yet the mattress was filled with the sticky redness that seemed to be streaming from between my legs. I feared I was dying. The flow went on for days, and so did my angst at what was happening to me. Then, I inexplicably stopped bleeding. Attempting to forget the incident, I struggled to turn the mattress over so I wouldn't see the blood and be reminded of that awful thought of doom.

But my dress, the same once-yellow dress I had worn while swinging on the tire swing that fateful day and every day since, was also covered in those brown blood stains. Looking at the worn fabric reminded me daily of all that I had been through. The rips from his aggression and the stench from both our bodies that clung to it were unwanted facts of life. But although I had grown, the dress had not. It didn't even cover my bum anymore, and it was very tight around my chest. Still, I didn't dare take it off. It was all I had to cover me.

The days passed, and I nearly forgot about the rush of blood. And then, to my horror, it happened again. This time, bringing with it aches in my whole body and crushing pain in my stomach. I pulled myself into a fetal position and held back the forbidden tears, not knowing what else to do. Not knowing what was happening or how to stop the pain or the bleeding. This time, there was simply no covering up the blood on the mattress.

Lying there, I heard his car coming toward the shack again. I shook, anticipating the pain of his body infiltrating mine. I couldn't bear the thought. He opened the door. I was too weak to move, and I didn't even care if he saw all the blood. He did. And then he slammed the door and left. I was sure he was leaving me to die.

But the blood eventually stopped again, leaving me more confused than ever, wondering what was happening to my body.

Days passed, and the repulsive sound of his car returning caused my stomach to lurch. I weakened as the car door slammed. But there was a sense of wonder as the thought washed over me that somehow he knew I wouldn't die despite my unexplained blood loss. Maybe he knew something I didn't.

My whole body tensed when he stumbled in the door with his disgusting smell surrounding him. He threw a bag at me before throwing himself on me, and then the pain rushed in. Once again.

Later, after he left, I opened the bag. Inside was my typical meal of peanut butter and crackers, but there was something else. I pulled it out—amazed at the softness. For the first time in years, I held a piece of clothing that was different from my once-yellow dress. Although it was worn, tattered, and stained, it was new to me. And it even looked like it might fit my growing body.

Jocinda

Daddy never gave us much—very little food, very little clothing, no comfort, and certainly not anything anyone could describe as love. One day, when I was still a young girl, he brought a woman home. I had no idea who she was. Her name was Shell. I think it may have been short for Michelle, but I don't know. They did a lot of drugs. She liked the crack as much as he did. It made me sick. He had never brought a woman home. He would be gone for days at a time; I thought maybe he had another family somewhere. But there he was with a woman.

She came to me one day and tossed a bag at me. She said it was from daddy. She said he wanted me to look better for his "friends."

So, she did know.

I had wondered if she knew, but how could she not? In the few weeks that she had been there, a different "friend" of my daddy came to see me every night.

The dress had blue flowers. She took me to the bathroom and showed me how to wash myself. She told me that I was about to get my period and what to do about it. I wasn't sure what she was talking about because I had bled many times before. A month later, I found out what she meant when Mother Nature decided to tell me I was a woman. What a joke.

Shell didn't stay long. It took about two weeks before daddy got mad and slapped her hard. I heard her fall and something break. It brought back painful memories of how he hurt mama. It scared me and Violet because we both knew he could do that to us. We hid in our little room. The door slammed, and Shell was gone as quickly as she had come.

Again, we were left alone with this monster.

Going Out

As I approached my teen years, the man's visits often got longer, lasting days at a time. After raping me, he would sit in my space on the mattress while I cowered in the corner, not daring to say a word. Eventually, needing his cigarettes or to go to the bathroom, he would go outside and come back smelling even more strongly of smoke and alcohol.

But as his supply of alcohol and cigarettes diminished, he devised a further plan to use me to sustain his habits.

During the day, he would leave for hours. I later figured out he was scoping out trailers, front porches, and backyards to find things we could steal. Then he would return and, with few words, give me sparse instructions, telling me I had a job to do.

He gruffly ordered me to "keep quiet no matter what" as he pushed me out the door and across the pathway to the car. My feet tangled up under me as I felt the earth beneath them and struggled to cooperate, fearing the bears that would appear from the darkness. He threw me in the car, slammed the door, and we sped off from the shack. I couldn't see much out the windows except for the moonlight.

On that first outing, we pulled up to a rickety trailer. With the gun in his hand, the man instructed me to get out, sneak through the shadows, and take the shoes, thermos, and lantern that were on the porch. Then, I was to get back to the car.

"Make it quick," he slurred.

I could tell he thought his plan was brilliant because I was small, young, and should have been able to move nimbly. But the truth is that it was difficult for me even to walk. My insides had been torn up again and again, and my muscles had atrophied while sitting in the shack for years and walking no further than a few steps at a time.

Fearfully, I obeyed, opening the door and pulling myself out of the car. This pain was different as my muscles tried to work in sync with each other. Willing my body through the shadows, I fearfully grabbed the items he wanted and returned to the car as fast as I could.

He was pleased with my success. And if there is one thing I learned through the years, it was that when he was pleased, when I didn't cross him, when I just shut up and did what he said, his gruffness would smooth out for a few minutes, giving me relief. My whole existence revolved around providing him satisfaction.

We drove back to the shack, where he shoved the gun into my side, forcing me again to my isolation, and then sped off in the car. Once more, I lay on the mattress, fearing the dark and the bears and not knowing when the man would return with the gun. In my mind, I had no choice but to remain in his control.

As the months passed, he got more and more brazen, putting me in even more challenging situations.

We would go out again and again. Always at night and always to places that he had scoped out in advance. Sometimes, I was forced to climb fences, shimmy through small spaces, or carry objects that were too heavy for me to handle easily. I lived in fear, being chased by barking dogs and running as fast as I could to escape the porch lights that would come on when I made any noise at all. It wasn't unusual for me to trip and fall or get cut and bruised from broken fences and barbed wire.

All so he could sell everything I stole to buy his alcohol.

There were times I was instructed to take toys that I so longed to keep. But those things were never for me.

Sometimes, after selling the items and getting his money, he would head straight to a bar, leaving me in the car. I would hide between the seats until he came back. There were nights when it was so bitterly cold I thought I would freeze to death, and there were nights when the car got so hot and stuffy I felt like I would suffocate.

But no matter how I felt, I knew not to make a sound or movement that might cause his anger to erupt, the curse words to come flying out of his mouth, and the gun to be shoved in my face.

I learned life was better when I pleased him.

Jocinda

*L*istening to how this woman with the nice shoes became a thief reminds me of when Uncle Frank snuck me out to go to the store.

He had come over so I could "work." When he was done with me, he started getting angry because he wanted some whiskey, but daddy was passed out on the couch with an empty bottle. Uncle Frank grabbed me by the arm and told me I could provide in more ways than one.

He took me to the store and told me that when he started talking to the man behind the counter, I was to put a bottle of whiskey in my dress and not drop it. My heart pounded as I saw him start to talk to the store owner. He took his time and made sure that the man was not paying attention to me at all. I saw him wave his hand slightly, like he told me he would do when it was okay, and I quickly took the bottle and slid it into the pocket of my dress.

As I walked toward the front of the store, I was sure I would be caught. It never even occurred to me that being caught meant police, and that could be my escape from daddy. I just didn't think that way.

Before we walked out, the store owner gave me a piece of candy. I didn't know what to say. Mostly because I was stealing from him and he was being so nice to me. Uncle Frank told me to say thank you, and I did. No man had ever been nice to me. I wasn't sure what he wanted from me for the candy. As we walked out, I put it in my pocket to save for Violet.

Uncle Frank walked me back to the house. Daddy was still passed out when we walked in the back door. Uncle Frank had drunk almost half of the bottle of whiskey before we got there. He stank of cigarettes, sweat, and alcohol. When we walked in, he said it was time for me to repay him for taking me out. I knew what that meant. I went to the bedroom, and he followed.

As we passed Violet's room, I gave her the candy.

Getting Caught

One night I'll never forget began with what had become our usual routine.

After the man raped me, he fell asleep on top of me; I lay still as I always did until he woke up. This time, when he rose, he was in a rage. He pulled me up and instructed me to get in the car. I knew what was happening—we were going out to steal again.

Carelessly, he sped off to an area that looked familiar. I knew we had been there before. He screeched the car to a halt as the headlights illuminated a toolbox on a porch. Then he growled orders at me to retrieve it. Stumbling through the dark, I grabbed a shovel and reached for the toolbox as a light came on inside the house. Catching my breath, I turned and ran back toward the car with just the shovel, knowing he would be angry but more afraid of the light.

I got into the car, which was already moving, and struggled to close the door while still holding the shovel. I was thrown around the back of the car as he drove more recklessly than even I was used to. We suddenly stopped when he hit a ditch, and then I remember seeing the blue and red flashing lights of a police car.

The policeman came to the driver's door and made the man get out.

The next thing I knew, I was pulled from the old station wagon and put in the back seat of the police car. They asked me what my name was. I started to whisper, "Dana," but then the man was shoved in beside me, and his eyes clearly told me to shut up.

We were taken to the police station, where we were put into separate cells that were right next to each other. We remained there for the night while the man was to sleep off his drunken state, and I was to remain quiet.

From behind the bars, I could see the policeman sitting at his desk and hear the man snoring in the next cell. I couldn't help but stare at the wall. Hanging there on the wall was a picture of me! The image of me smiling was printed on a big piece of paper with letters that formed words I couldn't read.

My mind returned to the day the picture was taken at Uncle Howard's and Aunt Mildred's. It felt like a million years ago, but I remember smiling so big for the camera while wearing my favorite dress and showing off my freshly cut bangs. Looking up at myself, I realized how much I had grown since that day. My hair was now below my butt—all snarly and matted. I didn't have shoes, let alone my favorite dress. And the smile on my face was long gone.

As I sat in the cell, I couldn't help but wonder why my picture was on the wall. But I didn't dare ask. I was deathly afraid of saying a word.

Many years later, I learned I had been looking at a "Missing Child" poster. And that missing child was me.

Morning came. The police officer took the man out of his cell and then came to take me out of my cell. We were driven back to the old station wagon. I was mesmerized by seeing the world in the light of day. Then we drove back to the shack like nothing ever happened.

But we only stayed there a night. The next day, my world changed again forever.

Jocinda

Missed chances. That's what the woman is talking about. Did she say her name was Dana? Dana and I both had so many missed chances.

What if she had just pointed to the poster on the wall so a cop would see it was her in the cell? How different would her life have been? All she had to do was tell the cops how the man had hurt her, and he could have helped. But she was so young. She just didn't know any better. I guess I wouldn't trust a cop, anyway.

But who can you trust to help? Thinking back now, how many times could I have grabbed Violet and run out the back door while daddy was passed out? Like mama did. How many times did I see one of the people on the street walking by outside that I could have screamed to please help me? Why didn't I ever tell anyone at school that my daddy was whoring me out for drugs and that he tried to kill my mama? They were all missed chances. Just like the woman had described.

But now I know why we both missed them.

Fear.

I lived in fear that my daddy would hurt us or kill us. And Dana lived in fear that the man would hurt or kill her. I was bonded to the woman in that way.

Pure, deep fear for our lives.

We didn't know just how close we could have been to being saved; the fear kept us right where we were. It kept us in a place where both of the men in our lives wanted us—too scared to ever say a word, even though our lives depended on it.

Her world may have changed forever, but I know the fear was still there. It had to be. Fear like that doesn't just go away.

On the Run

When I woke up the following day, the man ushered me to the car with his gun visible. I knew something was amiss because we were going out in the daylight. But of course, I did what I was told.

We drove for hours, passing fields and going through towns. During that time, he mentally abused me—threatening my life if I ever told anyone about what had been going on for all these years. Eventually, we crossed a state line. It wasn't until later that I realized we were actually fleeing from the police as he was now on their radar and didn't want his dirty secret, me, to be discovered. At the time, however, I had no idea why we were driving so far or where he was taking me.

We pulled into a service station for gas; the attendant smiled at me as he cleaned the windshield. My eyes were transfixed on him as I watched him moving purposefully. My captor dug into his pocket and pulled out change to pay the attendant, and we drove off again.

Once, he stopped on the side of the road and ordered me to get out. When I did, he pushed me into the weeds and told me that was my chance to go to the bathroom. Another time, we went into a store to buy some bread, which I was very thankful for. When we went inside, I knew not to speak; I couldn't anyway because of the rush of colors and people around me. I had grown so used to being alone in the dingy surroundings of the shack. While we were there, he led me to the bathroom and then stood outside the door on guard. As I sat down on the toilet, I vaguely remembered the feel of the seat, how to use toilet paper and even flush, as I had been taught so many years before. When I came out, he instructed me to stand outside a phone booth as he went in. I could hear him yelling at someone. I couldn't imagine who he was talking to, but he was as angry with them as he usually was with me.

After hours of riding in the car, we pulled up to an old farmhouse. We had been outside Flagstaff, Arizona, where the shack was, and now we arrived in Borger, Texas. He picked up his gun and said, "Git out. We're here. Keep your mouth shut. I don't want to hear your voice."

Following his commands, I got out, wondering what he wanted me to steal. But he got out, too, and pushed me inside the front door.

Jocinda

I've never been on a long car ride like that. Except for when they brought me here. But I was locked up even then, wearing handcuffs as I bounced along in the bus with all the other women they were bringing here.

I didn't know what would happen to me in prison.

I remember acting tough but being really scared. That's what you gotta do sometimes. Act tough so people don't know how scared you are.

I bet Dana knows what I mean.

A New Dwelling

We entered the house, and immediately in front of our faces was an unhappy woman who harshly said, "What ya doing in my house, Earl? Who's this vermin with ya?"

I'd never even thought about the man having a name before.

"Never you mind. We're here to stay, Mara. I'm hungry. Git me something to eat."

Earl pushed the woman aside and plopped down on the couch nearly on top of a girl who looked to be my age, snarling, "Git outta my way, Helen."

Helen got up from the couch and walked over to me. Taking my hand kindly, she led me to her bedroom. She had three younger brothers who came to see who I was—Earl Jr., Robert, and James. They were all very nice to me, asking me questions. But I didn't dare say a word, the phrase "Shut up or I'll kill you'" resonating in my thoughts.

As I sat on the bed, Helen brought me some clean clothes. "I know these are worn, but I think they'll fit ya. Ya oughtta take a bath before ya put 'em on. C'mon."

She led me into the bathroom, turned on the faucet, and out came warm water. She showed me where the soap was and handed me a worn but clean towel. Then she left me and said, "Whene'r yer done, I'll be in my room."

As she left, I looked at myself in the mirror. It was the first time I had seen my face in years. My skin was pale, and my hair was scraggly. I looked ugly. *Is this me?* I had changed so much from what I remembered.

Tears began to roll from my eyes, which I quickly blinked back. And I felt shame well up in me. I stuffed the feeling down inside and moved on, stepping into the bathtub.

The warmth of the water washed over me, trying to soothe my joints, but I couldn't relax for fear that the man…Earl…would come in and grab me at any moment. So I hurriedly washed myself as best I could and got back out. I put Helen's clothes on, which fit okay, and timidly opened the door.

I heard clanking in the kitchen and thought I must be dreaming when I caught a whiff of something cooking. Seeing Helen wave me back to her room, I stammered into the hall.

Instantly, I heard Earl yelling, "Where is she?" And in that flash of a moment, he appeared in the tiny hallway, grabbing my arm, pulling me next to him, and taking me into the kitchen. He pushed me into a seat and told me to stay there while Mara got the food.

Meanwhile, the other kids came in, looking at me but asking Mara if they could eat. Earl yelled at them to get out.

I watched what was going on, fearful of what would happen next and not understanding who these people were. Mara gave Earl a plate of food, which he gobbled down. He handed me a small piece of potato. I savored each precious bite despite the anxious churning of my stomach. The food was warm and cooked, making it the best meal I'd had in years.

Earl got up from the table. He put his hand on my neck and pushed me back to the room where Helen sat on the bed wide-eyed. Then, waving the ever-present gun, he grumbled "Git out" in Helen's direction.

Pulling a blanket off the bed and throwing it on the floor under the window, he told me that was where I would sleep. He lifted the window open and instructed me never to put it down. Then, he barked that his tapping on the window meant I was to crawl out and go to him. He reiterated I was not to talk or tell anyone about the things he did to me.

He left the room, and I dutifully lay under the window on the blanket. Fear kept me silent as I heard physical fighting between Earl and Mara from the other part of the small house. I listened, longing to hear the train whistle through the open window, but only fearing the sound of tapping. I knew he could now get to me at any moment of any day.

This was my new reality.

Jocinda

I didn't have a Helen in my life like the woman did, but I knew what it was to give to someone else. To try to provide for them.

My little sister Violet was so pretty and was everything to me—all I wanted to do was take care of her. She was the only family I ever had. She was my reason for living every day. So many times when daddy's "friends" would come, I honestly wanted to die. As I got older, I knew what they wanted, and it made me want to puke every time I saw one of them.

They were sick old men who abused and hurt young girls, but I was the one who felt dirty.

I got to the point where I didn't even think of it as rape anymore. It just was a thing that happened. It was the thing that HAD to happen so I could protect Violet. If they did it to me, they wouldn't hurt her. And if I let them do it, daddy wouldn't kill us.

That was my life. And that's what family does for each other.

I love Violet. I would protect her no matter what.

Trying to Fit In

The days at Mara's house grew long.

Playing with the kids outside became something I looked forward to. I was the oldest among the children. Helen was nine months younger than me, even though I was much smaller and scrawnier due to my lack of nutrition over the past years. On the days when the kids didn't go to school, we had a good time playing together outside. They even found a wheelchair to push me around in because I was unable to walk very well due to the excruciating pain brought on by my abuser, Earl, who I learned was their father.

As we spent time outside, the cellar was always there as a reminder of my primary service in the household. Whenever Earl beckoned, I would silently follow him down those dark steps.

Although the kids played in the cellar at times, it was not a fun place for me. The dirt floor, full of bugs and snakes in the dark dankness, spoke of adventure and intrigue to them. To me, it was a place of continued torture. Earl would take me there on a daily basis—sometimes several times a day—and often at night. If I didn't go willingly, he'd throw me down the steps onto the dirt floor. Every time he'd land his heavy body on top of mine. With the threat of the gun always present and the command to "Shut up," he would force himself on me time and again from the front and from behind, adding to my ongoing inability to walk without pain.

Thinking back on that cellar, I know there are so many details that have been wiped from my mind. The horrific acts that were inflicted on my entire body, physically, psychologically, and emotionally, were injuries that no person should have ever been able to heal from. But now I know I was protected. I had a purpose beyond the cellar. God had a plan for my life and ensured my ability to go on.

I never went to school, which I didn't question. I realized later that I was never seen as a person. To Earl, I was simply an object for him to do with as he pleased. To Mara, I was an outsider and an extra mouth to feed. And to the children, I was an oddity.

Besides not having developed physically, I had not learned any normal social skills beyond that of my five-year-old self. Because I was different, they all assumed I was stupid. My vocabulary had never expanded, and without use, there was much I had forgotten over my years in captivity and silence. My mouth was even unaccustomed to forming words, making it difficult for me to interact with them. I was slow to grasp what anyone else said or did, leading them to fits of laughter and cajoling at my expense.

As an adult, I can now understand that the children were reacting only to what they saw. They weren't able to recognize that they couldn't see the real me, but only a reflection of the trauma that characterized my life to that point. In reality, I was a prisoner held hostage by something more real than a gun or a shack.

I didn't know at the time that there was already a plan in place for me to be given complete freedom.

Days turned into weeks and weeks into months. My days and nights were marked by Earl's constant taps on the window demanding me to go to the cellar.

Besides being physically at his beck and call, I was also put in charge of watching over and feeding the other children when Earl and Mara would leave me, Helen, Earl Jr., Robert, and James in the house alone.

Food was scarce, but Helen and I did what we could to care for the boys. I remember going through the cabinets and finding whatever we could to cook. We didn't have much, but when the five of us were together and alone, I began to feel a warmth and satisfaction growing within me.

Playing outside released in me a joyful yet unfamiliar ease. I was awestruck to hear myself giggle. I loved watching James, the youngest, running from the tumbleweeds that would blow across the dirt yard. Once, during our innocent playtime, a new emotion grew within me. The children were playfully pushing me in my wheelchair behind the house near a ledge that dropped off into a dump yard. My wheelchair accidentally tumbled over the ledge, throwing me to the ground. I landed on broken glass and trash. The kids raced down to get me, picked me up, and helped me get cleaned up, nursing my wounds with their gentle hands. They were so kind and full of compassion that the joy in my heart overtook any pain my body should have been feeling at the time. They cleaned the blood splattered on my body, pulled the glass out of my legs and arms, and hugged me. I felt like I was no longer alone in this world.

Most days, the three older kids left for school early in the morning and returned in the late afternoon, leaving me alone with James, the youngest. I couldn't imagine what occupied Helen, Earl Jr., and Robert during those days, but with them gone, James and I developed a special bond. I was often responsible for his care, which was good. I loved his sweet smiles that pleasantly distracted me from my mundane daily chores, Mara's nasty gaze, and Earl's sickening addiction.

The only time Earl didn't bother me was when Mara was around. But when she was there, fights would inevitably erupt between them. This became a regular, frightening occurrence. The gun was always looming in sight, and often, they would throw furniture at each other, breaking it into pieces. I was caught in the crossfire of hate and anger. Much like the unusable pieces of wood that lie on the floor, no longer resembling furniture, I knew I was a damaged remnant of who I was meant to be. In the aftermath of the fighting, I would pick up the shattered pieces lying on the ground, wondering if anyone would ever be able to make them whole again. Or if anyone would ever be able to make me whole again.

When the children were home, I would try to shelter them from all the screaming and fighting. Earl was violent with Mara, but fortunately, he was not physically abusive toward the other children. The fighting would often get so bad that it became almost routine for the police to show up and take Earl to jail. What I remember most about the police was that when we heard the sirens in the distance, Earl would command me to run and hide. My go-to hiding place was the doghouse in the backyard, where I would stay quietly, waiting for things to calm down and the men with the unfamiliar voices to leave.

As it turns out, Earl was married to Mara and had fathered the other children. They were a family, and I was not part of it. As I watched Mara around the other children, I realized there was something very different in their relationship that I longed to have. Mara never offered me loving care or nurturing assurance. There were no hugs or touches of affection. Not once did I hear, "I love you, Dana. Sit on my lap."

My life was different now. I was no longer starving, and there were people around me.

But still, I was alone.

Jocinda

Hearing so many words pour out of the woman's mouth, Jocinda thought it odd that she had spent so many years unable to talk—being told to shut up and hide in the background. Jocinda could tell this woman was very smart; she sounded like she had gone to school, although she claimed she didn't.

There is something about her that I just can't put my finger on. She went through hell like me, but she came out on the other side. The man, Earl, hurt her and treated her like a dog. She even hid IN the doghouse. How messed up is that? She was his dog, but how did she get here?

As Dana continued to speak, Jocinda kept waiting to hear what changed.

Our lives were so much alike, but now we are so different. She is well dressed, smart, and speaking to a room full of criminals. I am a criminal. What or who made her who she was today? She lived in hell, but now she is okay.

I just don't get it.

Turning Point

One day, a day I remember as bright and beautiful, I was outside playing with the other children. Clothes were flapping on the clothesline in the gentle breeze, and the tumbleweeds were tumbling. That perfect scene was soon interrupted by Earl careening into the yard, his car skidding to a stop as the dirt flew. We all immediately got quiet and stepped back, watching as he jumped out, slammed the door, and aggressively approached me. Then, yelling at the other kids to go into the house, he shoved me toward the cellar.

Horror filled my being. *Will this never end?*

There I was, back on the dirt floor of the cellar, my tattered dress ripped off and lying on the ground; I shivered in nakedness, bracing myself for what I knew was next. Earl threw his unclothed body on top of mine and, with the gun in his hand, penetrated my mouth with his tongue, the pain below searing through me again.

Then, suddenly, the brightness of the sun illuminated the darkness. Earl jerked his head around, his pelvis brutally smashing harder into mine, piercing each of my nerves.

Mara had casually opened the cellar door. She was carefully descending the rickety stairs, focusing only on her next steps.

Earl froze as he continued to lay on top of me.

As Mara reached the bottom step, she instinctively raised her eyes, looking directly at us. Horror spread across her face. And all hell broke loose.

What happened next initiated a completely unexpected chain of events.

Mara screamed and ran back up the stairs. The sound of anger and betrayal in her wails hit my ears as she escaped the cellar and fled across the yard. Earl immediately jumped off me and grabbed his pants. He ordered me to shut up, shouting that he would kill me if I said anything—the same words I had heard over and over for so many years, but now even more direct and urgent than ever before. He snatched his gun, pulled on his pants, and bolted up the stairs, slamming the door behind him. I sat in silence, naked and not daring to move. Fearfully listening.

The next thing I heard was gunshots. I was petrified and had no idea who got shot or if Earl was coming back to kill me. My body trembled at the thought of his return in anger as I gasped to keep my own cries from erupting.

I don't know how much time passed as I sat there frozen. Then I heard the sirens. And they were coming closer. They got so close that I thought they would actually enter the cellar. I clutched my knees to my still-naked chest, waiting in the dimly lit dreariness, unable to move as I heard multiple car doors and unrecognizable voices.

Then the cellar door opened again as I cowered in the corner. An unfamiliar silhouette descended the stairs. When I wiped my eyes, I could tell it was a police officer. In a gentle voice, he said, "Honey, put your clothes on. We're here to take care of you."

He waited as I shakily stood up and walked over to my clothes lying in the dirt. I picked them up, put the dress over my head, and slid on my panties, and then I looked at him, afraid to say a word. He carefully led me up the stairs. As we came out of the cellar with the daylight blinding me, I saw chaos. There were police cars and ambulances and people in all kinds of uniforms.

Then, voices broke out near the drop-off behind the house, catching my attention. Several police officers were dragging Earl across the yard, blood covering his leg. They shoved him into a police car.

Next, Mara was brought from the house. She looked to be in a state of shock; there was blood on her as well.

I later found out that Mara had shot Earl. And Earl shot Mara.

I was put into a police car by myself. The other kids were put into a separate car. I never found out where they were taken.

Jocinda

They shot each other?

Jocinda almost had to laugh, but she didn't.

How many times had I wished someone would just shoot daddy and end me and Violet's suffering? All of them had guns. It was a way of life in the place we lived. All of them were either doing drugs, dealing drugs, or both. There were guns everywhere.

One time, while one of the men was on me, he was doing his business, and his gun fell out of his pants. It could have gone off and shot me, but it didn't.

So many times over the years, I wish I would have taken one of their guns and killed daddy. It's weird—I never thought about killing the others; I just wanted to kill him. The one who had put me through all this. The one who had tried to kill mama that night and changed my life forever.

There was such hate in my heart, I could never let go of it. It was black like the night and as deep as any ocean. No one could ever take this from me.

At the Hospital

We were met at the door of the hospital. They brought a wheelchair because I couldn't walk very well. As they pushed me down a hallway, I stared down at my bare, filthy, cut-up feet, noticing everyone else had shoes on. Everything around me was white and clean, and the lights were so bright.

They wheeled me into a room with a single bed. There were two women nurses dressed in white who helped me get up onto the bed. Then a male doctor, also dressed in white, came in and said he had to check me out. He told me to take off my clothes and told the nurses he had to do a "stirrup test" on me.

One nurse bravely spoke up, "You can't do that to her."

I listened, afraid to say a word and not understanding. The doctor replied that, by law, he had to make sure I didn't have a disease.

So, I obediently took my soiled dress off and sat there uncomfortably in that room with these strangers staring at me. What the doctor did next was so unexpected. First, he placed my feet in the stirrups and had the nurse scooch me down so my legs were bent in an awkward position. Then he pushed something big and cold and hard inside me, causing so much pain that I wanted to cry, but years of fear had taught me that I shouldn't ever cry. So I squeezed my eyes shut and tried to catch my breath.

When he was done, he looked at the nurse and said, "She will probably never be able to have children. She is brutally messed up—her insides are mutilated. Because of the severity of her abuse, she will certainly have serious mental issues."

Then he looked at me and said, "Those two you came in with are here. They have gunshot wounds and will need to stay for a while. But you can get dressed, and the nurses will take you to the front desk."

The doctor left, and one of the nurses looked at me with kind eyes as she carefully helped me put my dress back on and gingerly walked me to the front desk. I was confused as to where I would go since Earl and Mara were now in the hospital. But at the front desk, I was met by strangers who knew my name and told me to come with them.

Still not knowing where we were going, I allowed them to lead me out the door. When we stepped outside, I was startled by flashes of light and people yelling questions at us. The doctor who hurt me was answering the questions coming from the crowd as people stared at me.

"She's so messed up. She will never have children."

"No, she doesn't talk much. Her words come out very slowly—so she won't be able to answer any questions."

"This is just a case of poor white trash."

I stood there for what seemed like forever. Then, I was led through the crowd and continuous flashing lights to a car. I got in, and we drove away.

I had no idea those conveying my story were instigating an outpouring of care, compassion, and prayers that would affect my life. As I grew and entered this next phase, I regularly met people who told me they had heard my story. One woman who specifically prayed for me would later become a huge part of my life.

But at that moment, my thoughts were blurred. All I knew was we weren't returning to the now-familiar house with the tumbleweeds outside and the children playing in the yard. I had been yanked again from the only familiarity I knew.

Connecting Again

Dana looked out into the audience; her eyes focused again on Jocinda. Dana could see by the look on the woman's face and her body language that there was a story going on in her head. She breathed a prayer.

Heavenly Father, I pray for this woman you are impacting through my words. Reach her, Father. Reach her!

Dana's eyes locked with Jocinda's.

Jocinda

As her eyes locked with Dana's, Jocinda's mind reeled.

Why am I identifying with this woman? Our stories are very different. But why is there something here? There is something here.

Why does everything she says dig up my own memories I buried so long ago?

Nobody ever found me. I was never taken to a hospital or looked on by a nurse with kind eyes. I was stuck. I grew up stuck. And so did Violet.

Again, she thought,

How did I end up here while she ended up there? There has to be more to the story.

Much more.

In the Interim

The place they took me was different than anywhere I had been before. I spent much of my time in a big room that was packed with bunk beds and cribs. There was nothing fun there. I had my own bed, but the blanket they gave me was scratchy, and the air was stale. The floor, ceiling, and walls were bare cement, causing the cries of the other children who were in limbo with me to echo loudly.

I remember one particular baby who cried constantly. I would stand at her crib for hours with my hand on her, trying to soothe her. As her cries pierced through my heart, causing anxiety in me, I found myself yearning to hear the sound of the train that had always brought me comfort. Once, I asked an attendant why that precious baby would not stop crying. She responded, "She has been hurt, just like you." My heart skipped a beat when she said that, as emotion filled me. It was then that I realized that every child there had been abused, like me, and nobody knew what to do with us.

I was not allowed to watch TV, and when I asked why, they said there was massive news coverage all about me and my situation, and I needed to keep my mind clear for the trial. I didn't know what they meant or what a trial was, but who was I to question?

A man I didn't know visited me often. He was always dressed very fine, in a suit and tie, and had slicked-back hair. He asked me lots of questions and said he was my lawyer. I didn't know what that meant, but every time he arrived, the staff was very attentive and respectful to him. They went out of their way to find an empty room for the two of us to meet—usually an office with a couch on the second floor.

He asked me hard questions that I was not comfortable answering. For so many years, I had been ordered not to speak at all; now, here I was, being asked to tell another man everything Earl had done to me. The shame I had hidden for so long was now coming to light, and I didn't like it.

As I spoke in stilted language, the man, the lawyer, decided to help me along in my descriptions. He would touch me in the same places Earl had touched me and ask, "Did he touch you here?" "Did he do this?" I couldn't speak but merely nodded my head as tears welled up in my eyes. He did all the same things Earl did.

In this place where I was supposed to feel safe, I was again exposed and abused.

Then, the lawyer told me not to tell anyone how he touched me. He said no one would believe me anyway. And I knew he was right.

The day came when the staff told me to get washed up because it was time for the trial. The lawyer came and took me to his car, and we drove away. I didn't understand where we were going, only that I would need to answer the same questions I had been answering, but in front of other people.

We arrived at a large building. As we exited the car, men and women gathered all around—so many people that it scared me. The flashes of light were blinding as we walked through the crowd; they were yelling questions at me and the lawyer. *Are these the questions I am supposed to answer?* But my lawyer grasped my shoulders and moved me ahead of him—the touch of his hand sent shivers through my body.

This happened day after day. When we arrived, I was taken to a room where I would sit by myself. That always terrified me because I knew Earl was in the building, too. I knew this "trial" had something to do with him and what he had done to me.

One day, some official-looking men came to the room and took me to a larger room filled with people. They walked me to the front, where I had to sit behind a short wall facing everyone. There was a man sitting behind a big desk beside me. He was dressed in a long black robe. He looked at me with kind eyes and said, "Look straight at me. Don't look at the man in the orange suit."

I couldn't help but glance over at "the man in the orange suit," and I saw that it was Earl. When my eyes caught his, he mouthed, "I'll get you." He was still exerting control and causing the frightening dread I had known so very well from living with him those long years.

Then, the man in black asked me all kinds of questions about what Earl had done to me. I had a difficult time speaking, but he was patient with me. It was very quiet in that room full of people. I didn't dare look at Earl. I did look for Mara, but she wasn't there, and I didn't know why. I felt very distressed and alone.

After several days of going into that room and listening to different people speak and ask me questions, something different happened. Everyone stood quietly as the man in black entered the room carrying a little card. Not a sound could be heard as he read, "The jury finds this man guilty and sentences him to two years in prison." Then he leaned toward me and, looking over his glasses, said, "Your father won't be able to hurt you anymore."

My father?? The man in orange is called my father?

I didn't understand.

I later realized the brutal truth that Earl, the man who had abducted and abused me, was indeed my biological father.

Jocinda

*H*e was her father?

Jocinda's breath caught in her throat, and she felt a pressure in her chest as if someone was sitting on her. She couldn't believe it. This woman with the nice clothes, the shiny shoes, and perfect hair WAS like her. She had been betrayed, too. She had been used and treated like trash. By HER father.

Jocinda suddenly felt tears rolling down her face. She tried to remain stoic in that place where nobody dared show emotion, but she couldn't help herself.

Every memory and hurt boiled to the surface of her heart. She wanted to scream, but all she could do was cry.

I don't know her, but I know what she has gone through. And I hate her daddy as much as I hate mine.

I don't know how her story ended, but I know how mine did. That's why I'm here. And the hate I feel for the men who tortured us both is deep and black.

Then Jocinda realized something remarkable.

I'm feeling something else, too. I feel a connection to this woman like I've only felt for one other person in the whole world.

Violet.

My Next Home

In a trance, I was led outside the building, where the blinding flashes and yelling voices were again directed at me. We walked through the crowd to an opening where, to my delight, I saw children. I recognized them! It was Helen, Earl Jr., Robert, and James. My unease melted. I was just so happy to see them.

But my joy was interrupted when something happened that has been seared in my memory since that day.

I quickly made my way toward little James, who was running in my direction. I was so excited to gather him in my arms, but before we reached each other, an officer scooped him up and carried him away from me. The precious boy who always had a smile was now bellowing my name as tears ran down his face. The officer tried to console James, promising to give him many toys, but James responded by kicking and trying to get away.

I lunged toward the little boy who meant so much to me, my heart bursting with compassion, but my lawyer restrained me. The policeman who held James in his arms put him in his police car and tried to coax and calm him down by handing him a teddy bear, which James wanted nothing to do with. The official-looking man in charge then closed the car door, and I could no longer hear my sweet James screaming. I could only see his sorrowful face as he pressed his hands against the window as they drove off. To this day, it still breaks my heart to think of the last time I saw my James. That moment is a tragic picture frame that haunts my mind.

I stood, shell-shocked, with Helen, Earl Jr., and Robert.

Before long, a big white van pulled up. Two men got out and said they were with the Boys Ranch. The adults who were with us told Earl Jr. and Robert to say goodbye to Helen and me. We were all too stunned to speak. The boys walked to the van, escorted by the adults, and reluctantly climbed in as they were instructed. Then, the van drove away.

I would never see them again.

A few minutes later, a station wagon pulled up. This time, Helen and I were instructed to get in. We didn't know our next destination, but we were relieved that we were at least leaving together. Still exasperated, my body heaved with sobs of grief thinking about the fact that the five of us, my half brothers and sister and me, would never again play and laugh together in the yard with the tumbleweeds.

Helen cried uncontrollably. I sat there bottling my feelings up as I always did. Still, tears made their way down my face as we rode in silence in the back seat. Eventually, we pulled up to Amarillo Children's Home in Amarillo, Texas, where we would begin our next chapter.

When we arrived, Helen and I were escorted through a maze of hallways to a room with three beds. We were told that was where we would stay. Later, we met our new roommate when she returned from school.

In the coming days, we were given time to get acclimated to our new place, but then we were suddenly jolted from our surroundings yet again.

Just a few days after we arrived, we were called to the office and told we would be driven back to the hospital because the kids' mother, Mara, was dying.

Helen and I didn't speak much on the way. When we arrived, we were led to Mara's hospital room, which was very much like the one I had been in after they found me that last time in the cellar. Flashes of the pain that the doctor inflicted on me surfaced in my mind, but I pushed those thoughts away, as I had become accustomed to doing.

We walked into Mara's room. She was in an oxygen tent, and I noticed how skinny she was. She couldn't speak, but she wrote a note that said, "I love you." Oh, the pain we felt as we watched her take her last breath.

Now everything had been taken from us. First, our three brothers, and now, Mara. Even though she was never really nice to me, somehow I was able to appreciate the traumatic circumstances of her life. Despite Earl's daily infliction of abuse, Mara never stopped being a mother to her children. I was learning that being able to care for someone else is a gift we receive. And no one can interfere with that assignment in our life.

We were driven back to the children's home. That night, I lay in my bed feeling so much guilt and pain. I wondered what would have happened if I hadn't come into Helen's life. Would her family still be a family? Now Helen had nothing. Her brothers were far away, her mother was dead, and her father was in prison.

Jocinda

They were separated. That was a feeling I knew all too well.

As this woman talked about seeing James pulled away from her, I could only think of Violet. We, too, had been pulled apart. But I had known it was coming because of what I did. That night came back to my mind along with all the feelings that lived with it. I had pushed all of it down. I knew I had to swallow it, or it would eat me up. Still, it was there. It would always be there.

Terror.

Anger.

Relief.

And then unimaginable grief.

It started with Uncle Frank. I was 18, and he came to do what he always did. By that time, I was numb to it. He came, did his business, paid daddy, and left. It happened every week, often on a Friday when he got his paycheck. He was usually drunk or high or both. Sometimes, he was so out of it he couldn't even finish what he started. I would just lay there and let him try, and sometimes, he would pass out on top of me.

I will never forget that one Friday.

It was a cold night. And it was raining. That kind of winter storm that is loud and nasty. Uncle Frank showed up, and I could tell he was in a bad way. His eyes were *two different sizes, and his breath smelled of cheap whiskey. He came in, and I could tell it was going to be a quick visit, thank God.*

He got undressed but couldn't even get his pants off. He just let them fall to the floor and got on top of me. He couldn't do it, but he tried and tried. While he was on me, I heard something fall to the floor. It was a dull thud like metal on wood. I heard it. But he didn't.

After a while, he got angry because he couldn't finish. He pulled up his pants and said I wasn't good anymore. I was too old. He called me ugly. I started to stand up, and he shoved me back down on the bed. He stumbled out of the room.

I started to get dressed, reaching down on the floor to get my shoes.

That was when I saw the gun.

It had fallen out of his pants when he was on top of me. That was the thud I heard. It was just under the edge of the bed, and I reached for it. It was much heavier than I expected. I would later learn it was a .22 caliber pistol. It was called a Saturday Night Special, but I never learned why.

I heard voices from the other room. Uncle Frank had not left; he was yelling at daddy. Daddy was yelling back. They were arguing about me. Frank told daddy I was "no good no more" and that I "wasn't worth nothin no more." He said I wasn't worth paying for.

They started to fight, and I was scared.

Uncle Frank had been to the house many times, but nothing like this had ever happened. I was afraid to leave the room; I knew it was bad. I wanted to get to the bedroom where Violet was, but I was too scared to open the door.

Then I heard something crash and more yelling. Uncle Frank yelled that he was going to kill daddy. I knew he was looking for his gun. The same gun that I was holding in my hand. I hid it under the pillow, fearing he would come looking for it. I heard the front door slam and more yelling.

I was about to leave to go to Violet. As I reached for the doorknob, daddy threw the door open. He had a wild look in his eyes. It was the same look I had seen in him the night he beat mama and told her he would kill her. My heart was beating so fast that I thought it would explode out of my chest. I don't know that I have ever been that scared before or since.

Daddy slapped me hard. I felt blood start to come out of my nose. His blow had knocked me back on the bed. He pulled his belt off and started to hit me with it. The leather stung my legs and back. I thought he was going to kill me, and I didn't even know why. He screamed it was all my fault. I would later learn that Uncle Frank had refused to pay him. He told daddy I was no good and I was used up. Daddy turned his anger towards me because he didn't get his money.

Daddy said I was just a used-up whore and that I couldn't make him money anymore. He yelled as he swung the belt. I tried to scream, but all I could manage was a whimper. I was face down on the bed, trying to shield my face as he hit me. Then, for no reason at all, he stopped. I turned and looked at him. He was bleeding where Uncle Frank had hit him in the mouth when they fought.

Then, with a sinister smile, he said since I was used up and no good, he knew his friends would pay good money for a virgin.

I immediately knew he meant Violet.

This horrible monster was going to do to her what he had done to me for years. He was going to lock her in the same hell where he had forced me to live my life.

I don't remember my fear turning to anger, but it did. It was white hot. All the years of abuse, neglect, and starvation came to the surface in one moment. I couldn't let him do it. I had sworn to protect Violet. He said he was going to go "try her first" right then.

I reached under the pillow and felt the handle of the gun.

I turned and pointed it at him. I was shaking, not from fear, but from all-consuming anger.

He asked me what I was going to do—shoot him? He said I didn't have it in me and that I was weak. He said I was going to pay forever for threatening him. He raised his fist and lunged at me.

The sound was deafening.

I felt the gun jump in my hand as I pulled the trigger.

The bullet tore through his chest, and I could smell the gunpowder. The force of the impact pushed him back, and he fell to the floor.

I scrambled to the edge of the bed and saw him lying there. He was coughing blood. I pointed the gun and shot him again. The second shot killed him. His body twitched, and then he was gone. I saw the life go out of his eyes.

I dropped the gun to the floor, and I knew it was over.

Then I saw Violet standing In the doorway. She had seen it all.

Who Is Able?

The night Mara died, I lay in bed in the children's home in total darkness, wanting to cry more than I ever had before. Even though Helen and our roommate were asleep beside me, my eyes saw only emptiness, a room with nothing surrounding me. So much pent-up emotion was afflicting me, and I knew it had to be released somehow. Everything was confusing. My world, as I knew it, had been shaken. The darkness was not a welcome companion. I felt oh so alone, abandoned once again.

I had always kept everything in, but it was as if these last days had caused an eruption of grief and pain inside me that tried to come spilling out. Every muscle in my body was tense and shaking. I was so cold, and my head was pounding. It was as if my whole body wanted to explode. Even though I no longer feared hearing the terrifying sounds of the car driving up on the gravel or the tapping on the window signaling my oncoming abuse, it was as if every horrible emotion I ever felt, or refused to feel, was bubbling up inside me. And yet, somehow, I was empty. Knowing I would never experience the comfort from the distant sound of the train or the laughter of the children as we played together, I was lost and alone. So alone.

In my mind, I screamed into the darkness. *How can I go on? Where will I find comfort? What have I done to deserve the abuse that brought me here? What does it even mean that Earl is my father? Who is my mother? What is wrong with me? What will happen to me? At this point, who will ever be able to help me?*

Suddenly, out of the gut-wrenching night, a brilliant radiance pierced the darkness. At first, I thought the housemother had turned on the bedroom light, but then I realized it couldn't be that. It was the most intense, whitest illumination I'd ever seen.

I rolled over to streams of brightness all around me, as tall as the ceiling above me. Stunned with awe, I was pulled out of my misery as I saw the astonishing presence of an angel in front of me. The magnificent being looked directly at me with penetrating eyes and extreme comfort and said, "Jesus loves you and will always be with you!"

Instantaneously, a flood of peace encompassed me. Miraculously, my body released all the tension it was holding as warmth permeated every cell of my body. I had never before experienced or imagined such immense joy as what flowed through me at that moment. I wiped my face, recognizing that my fear and anger were now gone—along with the pain, loneliness, and questions about my future.

The angel said words I didn't understand but didn't question. "Jesus loves you and will always be with you." I didn't know who Jesus was. And even though I had never heard that name and didn't know what love was, I immediately understood that both were filled with power and goodness. Strength and comfort laced with hope infused me.

As the bright light faded and I drifted into a peaceful sleep, a smile remained painted on my face. I couldn't wait to discuss with Helen in the morning what I was sure we had both seen that night. I will never forget that divine encounter for the rest of my life. It would carry me through a future of uncertainty, constantly reminding me that there is far more destined for my life than I could possibly understand.

I awoke in the morning, still full of exuberant joy and eager anticipation to speak with Helen. I lay in bed, just waiting for her to open her eyes. When she did, she looked at me groggily. Immediately, I began rambling on about the light that had taken over the room, the words the angel spoke so clearly and kindly, and the unforgettable peace still filling me. I didn't stop to take a breath. I don't think I had ever spoken that many words at one time before. But I couldn't stop.

When I finally paused, I noticed Helen's wide eyes and gaping mouth. She had no idea what I was talking about! She continued to stare at me, motionless. Suddenly, I didn't know what to say next.

So I got up, still carrying my excitement, and went about my day, undeniably knowing things would be different for me going forward.

Jocinda

Things became different for me, too, but not in a way that was good, like the woman. I didn't have no angel to tell me everything was going to be alright. I didn't feel any peace or see any bright light. The only lights I saw were from police cars.

The neighbors had called the police when they heard the fight between Uncle Frank and daddy. They were on the way when I killed him.

I heard the sirens and knew they were coming for me. I took Violet by the hand and walked into the front room. There was a big cop with his gun pointed at us. He could see daddy on the floor behind us. He asked who shot him, and I said I did.

He told me to get down on my knees. And I did. Violet started to, but he took her hand and pulled her behind him. Another cop took her outside. He asked me where the gun was, and I told him it was on the bed.

I still remember how cold the handcuffs were and the sound they made as he put them on my wrists. He pulled me to my feet and walked me out the front door. I could see Violet in a police car. I thought they would put us in the same car, but he was walking me to a different one. Violet put her hand on the window of the car she was in; I could see she was crying.

I will never forget thinking that our lives had changed forever. But I had to do it to protect her.

When he put me in the car, I breathed a sigh of relief. I knew I was going to jail, but at least Violet would be free and safe.

Early School Days

Helen and I began establishing a routine and settling into our new home. As all the children attended school, we knew we would soon be put into the system. For Helen, the idea of going to school seemed to be a source of comfort. She felt as if she was returning to a bit of normalcy. But for me, even thinking about school was daunting and frightful as I had no idea what to expect.

I was put into the fifth grade based solely on my age, despite the fact I couldn't read, write, or even comfortably speak to an adult. I didn't know simple math or the names of things or even my ABCs. I was self-conscious, and rightfully so. I couldn't help but feel that all the kids could see how dumb and backward I was. They certainly didn't hide their opinions about me.

I struggled so hard, having absolutely no prior schooling or teaching of any kind. My days felt like I was trapped in a torture chamber. If there was one thing I had learned, however, it was to endure suffering and obediently follow commands I was given. Regularly, my body reacted to the stress with extreme tension that caused me to clench my fists and block out everything around me. This coping mechanism was one I had learned and perfected through many hours of enduring both physical and psychological pain on that dirty mattress and dusty cellar floor under the weight of Earl's body as he abused me.

In the classroom, the teacher would often call on me, but I never could respond to the question. Besides not having the answer, my voice was stifled by fear. So, the teacher's strides to instruct and include me had the opposite effect than intended, which infected me with deeper feelings of shame and embarrassment. I always felt a total blank in my head, and I had learned years earlier that feeling or showing emotion wasn't worthwhile. Not for me, anyway. Tears were useless, as were anger and frustration. Instead, I coped by holding everything in. I just sat silently, clenching my fists.

As the anxiety within me built up, I would often black out. My mind would shut down as I entered into a darkened chasm of nothingness, overcome with fear and panic. I experienced feelings so intense I literally could not see or hear anything. I can't imagine now what the teachers must have thought as I sat in a catatonic state, unable to respond. Periodically, I would be startled to attention by the laughter from the kids around me. School days were rough days.

I was so uncomfortable around the other girls and boys my age. It was awful knowing that these kids could plainly see my awkwardness and how far behind I was, yet they didn't care enough to know anything about why I was who I was. Not one of my classmates took the time to recognize my value, worth, feelings, or insecurities. I was approached by the school principal, who noticed my unease. When asked if I was okay, I simply shook my head yes, not daring to reveal the darkness I truly felt.

I don't remember ever having any friends at all. Instead, I continually faced more rejection, feelings of loneliness, and lack of acceptance because I just didn't fit in. No one liked me. No one wanted me. All I experienced propelled the lie I believed from early on in my life that something was wrong with me.

Living at the home only added to my disengagement at school.

I began to recognize the divide between me and my classmates—who would have nothing to do with me and with whom I had nothing in common. I had no parents, no house to call home, no friends, and no previous schooling.

Another defining difference between us was the way I dressed. People from the community would graciously donate clothes for the children living in the home. The donations were kept in the basement, and on occasion, we would be taken downstairs to try them on. We would rummage through the boxes of old clothes that were worn and out of style, just looking for something that would fit. It always seemed like anything that fit me was the ugliest thing there. As I grew, how I looked became a source of embarrassment. It was pointed out to me that when I walked, I would clutch my shirt near the neckline with my fist clenched, stretching it out and making my appearance even more disheveled.

Learning was so difficult as I was so far behind. Most of my teachers had no patience with me, but I had one teacher to whom I owe so much. One teacher who cared. He would invite me to stay after school with the intended purpose of helping me with my studies. But what that teacher did for me was so much greater than he probably ever understood. He took me under his wing and helped me grow emotionally.

His kindness and guidance strengthened me as he began to gently pry open the vault of excruciating pain and emotion that had grown inside me over the years. During the precious time he spent tutoring me, I learned what it meant to trust someone, a feeling that was quite foreign. I had never experienced such ongoing care and concern from anyone. I even felt comfortable enough to tell him about some of the things that had happened to me. He listened intently and with compassion, instilling in me a confidence that allowed me, for the first time, to feel that I was a somebody.

Although the special attention from that one teacher changed my perspective and helped my learning improve, my grades were still not what everyone thought they should be. Mother Mae, who looked after us at the home, was not shy in telling me that learning the basics of math and reading would be a skill I would probably never be able to master. And though she brainwashed me with her belief that I would never amount to anything, she still held me accountable. Each time she saw my report card, she would take out a ping pong paddle covered with duct tape and paddle me—making sure I understood that my attempts at learning were failing.

Still, as I matured and grew from each circumstance, I learned to find glimpses of joy. One of my favorite pastimes was caring for the younger children in the home. I loved watching them as they responded to my tenderness. Often, they would come into the home sullen and filled with distrust. I would approach them with a smile and affection, soothing them when they cried and helping them adjust to their new surroundings. It was unusual for me not to have a little one at my side.

Sometimes, a nice couple would come into the home looking to adopt a child. Inevitably, they would be drawn to the young ones who had found a sense of belonging and peace in my presence. I don't know if it was because they were young or that their eyes were brighter than the other children's, but often, those who stuck by my side were the very children who were selected to be adopted. My heart soared at the prospect of my sweet friends being granted a forever home, but the ache of losing them was always present.

As the kids left with their new parents, I often wondered what it would be like to be wanted. I kept hoping that someday I, too, would have a family.

Jocinda

She was learning to trust people. Maybe that's what is different about us. I quickly found out that everyone was against me.

My trial was a joke. I got a white public defender who had too many cases already, and I was just a black girl who had shot and killed her daddy, a black man. He didn't even seem to care about what had been done to me.

He said I had killed the only person who could prove I had been mistreated. And he said that because Violet was a minor and my sister, no one would believe her anyway.

The trial took all of one week.

I was convicted of manslaughter because daddy had been beating me at the time I killed him. I was sentenced to 15 years, which was the maximum in Michigan.

I was going to be in prison for the same amount of time that I had been used.

Molested Along the Way

Life became routine, consisting of school, meals, and chores. I picked up bad habits, including foul language. Obscene words, spoken to me through years of abuse, became part of my regular speech. In my daily frustration, I used shocking phrases in a feeble effort to express my emotions. This did not go over well with the house mom, who hauled off and slapped me across the face when I spat the b-word behind her back.

Still, the mundane drudgery was preferable to the abuse that continually tried to destroy my life.

Is there something about what I am doing or who I am that makes so many men want to molest me? Questions rose up inside of me, but without anyone to ask or care, I accepted my circumstances.

Often, men I was left alone with for various reasons would make sexual advances towards me. As I grew and became more aware of my body as a developing woman, the sexual abuse that came at me from all angles was even more disconcerting than it had been when I was a little girl. This abuse happened often, as if it was following me through my life. Men continued to exert such control over me, and I began to grow more and more afraid. Great fear continued to be my unwanted companion as I experienced feelings of dread and horror that came along with having no command over what was being done to me.

Will I ever be free from this?

The jagged edges of my daily treatment pierced my soul. Before I knew it, the unthinkable happened, tearing open the casement of painful memories I had pushed deep within me.

Earl was released from prison.

And because he was my biological father, he was now permitted to come and visit me on a regular basis. Unbelievable! He hadn't changed one bit. His access to me once again brought a whole new realm of insecurity.

Once a month, after we returned from church, friends and family were welcomed to visit the children at the home. Certain rooms were set aside for visitation to provide the visitor and child privacy. Because it was Sunday and all the girls were required to wear dresses to church, those who were "lucky" enough to have visitors would already be dressed up.

So, once a month, I had no choice but to allow Earl to lead me to one of the secluded rooms. My stomach would tie in knots as we entered the private space and he closed the door, cutting me off from any source of protection. I was alone again with Earl, the dress giving him easy access to my body. This very same man who had a record of previous crimes against me was again granted the authorization to harm me further.

Periodically, someone from the home would check on us, but that did not stop Earl from touching me inappropriately, including the sensual kissing and penetration he forced upon me, lifting my dress as that familiar pain once again seared through my body, causing me to clench my fists and retreat into my mind to block the anguish.

Oh, the torment. Earl was still exerting his awful ways over me.

Who would ever be able to protect and rescue me?

Jocinda

I can understand being locked in a room and not being able to get away.

That is my life now.

This place is hell. Early on, I learned that once you are a victim, you will always be easy prey. And what has been done to me by a parade of nasty men who looked at me like a "thing" instead of a person is nothing compared to what women can do. Prison women are brutal.

There are gangs in here. And either you are in one, or you get abused by all of them. I've tried to stay clear as much as I could, but it's no use. The guards sure don't care. I am a castaway, a piece of gutter trash, and they just look the other way.

I was abused more in my first week here than I had been in a month at daddy's. It was never just one at a time, either. They run in packs like dogs. They don't care. They humiliate me, abuse me, spit on me, and all manner of degrading things.

So many times in my previous life, I just went silent and retreated to that place in my head where no one could hurt my spirit while the men used my body. Here in prison, I've had to use that skill again over and over. Finally, I gave in and joined a gang of women just for a measure of protection. At least, that was what I thought. In prison, the way you show your loyalty is to use others but let your gang use you.

It is torture. It is hell.

And it is my life every day.

Introduced to Love

Entering high school brought many changes. At the outset, I experienced the normal transition of the chaos of dealing with so many teachers, all of whom expected me to organize homework and notebooks, which I had no idea how to do. On top of that was the confusing array of social activities that were part of the atmosphere around me. Like most high school students, I was struck by how difficult the advanced levels of learning were. But in my case, I also had to deal with the ongoing struggle of not knowing even the basics of reading and writing. Despite my best efforts, I still could not catch up.

Many people throughout my lifetime would later ask me, "How did you graduate, Dana?"

"Nobody knows," was my reply. Nevertheless, I somehow made it through high school and received my diploma.

After I graduated and turned seventeen, I was forced by the state to move out of the children's home. Unable to be on my own—with no money, no self-esteem, and no plans for a future—I moved to live with a foster family who offered to take me in.

That is when my life took another unexpected turn: Gene's family stepped in. I had met Gene at a local dance while I was still in high school. From that first moment, I was drawn to him like a magnet. I knew something different was happening, although I couldn't understand what it was. Something propelled me to his side and enabled me to open a conversation with strength and poise I didn't know I had. I liked him. I really liked him. And besides that, he was cute.

We began hanging out. He cared about me in a way I hadn't experienced before. I felt safe in his presence, and somehow, I was able to accept the tenderness that he showed me. Even his physical touch was welcome, which is astounding to me to this day, as all prior touch to my body had been abusive and invasive. I found myself giving in to the feelings between us and ended up getting pregnant.

We were so young and didn't know what to do. Gene's parents were very kind and trustworthy, and Gene felt it best that we should confide in them. When we did, they welcomed me into their family with open arms. Gene's mother already had six children whom she loved, but she made room in her heart for me, taking me in as one of her own. She was the sweetest, most loving, nurturing woman that ever was. She never complained or had a mean word to say about anyone. I wanted to be just like her when I grew up.

Gene's parents counseled us to get married, which we did, and I moved into their home. I was just 18 years old and had never heard or said the words "I love you." I had yet to learn what love really meant. Gene often expressed his love for me, leaving me in silence—unable to respond. I couldn't say what I didn't understand.

Over the years, I've learned how vital it is to verbalize love to others, and to this day, it still hurts me that as our marriage began, I couldn't tell my husband "I love you, too."

Wanting to share who I was, I told Gene about my abusive past, and I trusted him with bringing this information to his parents. Not only was it right to tell my story, but living in a small town, I figured they had heard about me from the radio, TV, and newspapers. And I was right. Gene explained my past, and later, as we discussed it openly, Gene's mom revealed that she had prayed for me, the little girl with such a big story.

Their acceptance began a transformation that set me on a new trajectory. Suddenly, I was more than "that little girl with the abusive father." I was Dana—a wife, a daughter-in-law, and a soon-to-be mother. And I began to understand the feeling of being loved.

Jocinda

A man who loves you. What must that be like?

I have no earthly idea.

There has never been a man in my life who loved me. More than that, I can't even remember one who didn't hurt me. I never saw a man smile in a way that didn't mean he wanted me for what he could do to my body. I sure know what to expect when I see a nasty snarl spread across a man's face directed at me. There have been times when I've seen married people who look happy. I've never really understood that.

Trying to explain love to Jocinda was like trying to tell someone who never saw the ocean what it was like to see, feel, smell, and hear the crashing waves. How can you understand something you've never experienced? Jocinda just couldn't relate to how Dana's heart began to open. No. Jocinda had always lived in fear and couldn't begin to comprehend that people are made to love and trust others. There wasn't even a crack in her exterior that allowed her to imagine letting any light in.

But as she listened, perhaps there was a glimmer of hope after all. Sometimes, hope can be ignited by someone else's story.

Hearing this woman tell her story makes me wonder what it must be like to have someone who cares about you and puts you first. Someone who wants the best for you and makes sacrifices for you. Someone you could trust unconditionally and would love you back...unconditionally. Someone like that man Gene.

I've thought about that before. It's usually at night when those kinds of thoughts float into my mind. Like when I'm lying in my bed listening to my heartbeat, and I hear that small voice in my head speaking to me.

Here in prison, you have a lot of time to think. I know a lot of people don't like that, but I do. But when my little voice tells me about things like relationships, I laugh to myself. A relationship ain't in the cards for me. That's for a different kind of folk.

I bet the lady on stage and her husband have a nice house. Maybe by now, she has a whole family. I bet they all sit around a table for dinner and hold hands for a prayer—I've seen people like the Waltons do that on TV. No matter what that voice in my head says, though, I know I will never have those things. Not after what I have been through. I'm not like her. I'm damaged. I don't get second chances to have a good life.

But I guess that's what a normal life is—having someone who loves you, kids, and a big house. Love and security.

I'm not normal; I could never be normal like that.

And as sure as me and this woman have been through some of the same things, we are different. We could never be the same.

Early Days of Marriage

The responsibilities of being a husband and a soon-to-be-father became Gene's reality. He took his role of becoming a provider seriously and began a hefty load of shift work. Having him gone at random times throughout the day and night made it difficult for me as I tried to figure out what my world should look like in Gene's absence.

Gene's mom was always a bright spot. As the hub of all the activity happening in the household, her grace and care amazed me. Always looking outside herself and her needs, she was so in tune with what each individual needed—even me. She was the epitome of selflessness.

Having never experienced a nurturing mother or a healthy family lifestyle, I soaked up the atmosphere like a sponge. Not only did I see a beautiful example of what a wife could be, but with wonder and awe, I also witnessed the effects of being—and having—a dedicated mother. Her warmhearted and tireless devotion to her family showed me the exuberant joy that daily life could bring.

As I shadowed my new mentor in her household duties, learning how to be a good wife and mother, my fear of having a family to take care of began to fade. For the first time, I began to see that I had control of the decisions ahead of me. The health of Gene's family taught me to trust that I had the ability to choose the direction of my life.

Then, just as Gene and I began making headway toward our goal of preparing a home for our budding family, devastation struck.

One day when I was in my second trimester, while Gene was at work, I woke up in excruciating pain and lying in a puddle of blood. Not understanding what was happening, I yelled for Gene's mom. She was immediately by my side and knew exactly what to do. Without hesitation, she took me to the hospital.

I couldn't help but think I was losing my baby.

Through the whole ordeal, the words that echoed in my brain were those of the doctor who had first examined me after I was rescued: "She will probably never be able to have children. She is so brutally messed up—her insides are mutilated."

But despite my years of abuse, I HAD gotten pregnant. Still, that doctor seemed to have been right. The evil, which had already robbed me of so much, wasn't finished torturing me.

After arriving at the hospital, I underwent an array of examinations and procedures. Too stunned to react to what was happening, I gave myself over to the care of the medical staff.

Still, there was no denying what was happening.

Our heartbreak became deeper as Gene and I received the definitive news that our babies were gone. We didn't even know I had been carrying twins. It felt like just one more blow to my already battered heart.

As I prepared to leave the hospital, my doctor spoke words that triggered more pain and haunted me for years to come: "You will never be able to carry a child to full term."

Gene's mom was so loving and comforting, holding me up while teaching me about the power we each wield in each other's lives. The support I received from her allowed me to begin to recognize that I also have something beautiful to give.

I finally told Gene, "I love you."

Jocinda

Again, Jocinda felt a spark of kinship with this woman on the stage. They both knew unspeakable fear, and, now she understood, they both knew unfathomable loss.

Jocinda had caught her breath as the woman described the pain of losing her child. There is a bond between parents who have lost children.

Jocinda felt Dana's heartache all too well.

I was pregnant once. I don't even know who the daddy was. It could have been Uncle Frank, but there was no way to tell. Some men used condoms, but a lot didn't. And I couldn't tell them no. I just hoped they were clean. It's amazing I never caught anything from them.

I didn't get a disease, but I did get a baby. Well, almost.

I was young and didn't know much, but I knew something wasn't right. My period stopped, and I started to feel sick nearly every day. I think daddy suspected but didn't want to admit it. I was just a tool to him. Something to sell and make money.

There was a lady who lived next door. I don't know what her real name was, but everyone called her Queenie. She was older and had dark skin, deep brown eyes, and a gentle smile. If I had known my grandmother, I hoped she would be like Queenie. Daddy asked her to come over one day and told her I was sick. He said he thought I had "female problems." Queenie had no idea what he did to us. She didn't mess in other people's business.

When Queenie came over and looked at me, she knew right away. My stomach had started to swell. I hadn't really thought anything about it until she ran her wrinkled hands over my belly. She asked me a few questions and then turned to daddy.

"She ain't sick. This girl is pregnant."

Daddy's anger was all over his face. I am sure that Queenie thought it was because I was pregnant and there was no husband, but I knew the truth. Daddy wanted me to keep "working."

Queenie told daddy I needed to go to a doctor and get checked out, or the baby might not come out right. She offered to take me to the clinic over on Celestine Street. Daddy told her he would take care of it. I didn't know what he meant, but I was scared. Nothing he ever did was good, and he sure never took care of anything when it came to me and Violet.

Queenie left. Daddy watched her through the window as she walked down the steps to the street. I just stood there thinking. My head was spinning. I was 15, and I was gonna be a mama. In my mind, I started to think what that would mean. Maybe daddy would leave me and Violet alone. Maybe having a grandbaby might make him happy, and he would change. What if I had a little girl? I knew I could make her have a better life than mine. Anything would be better than mine. Me and Violet would love her and take care of her. We could be her parents and love her. We would make her feel special, feel like she mattered. I finally had something to smile about.

Jocinda winced as she remembered what happened next.

My feeling of excitement sure didn't last long. It was shattered by a hard slap that pushed me back into the kitchen wall. Daddy screamed that I was stupid for "letting some damn man knock you up." I fought to hold back the tears that welled up in my eyes. My face stung where he had hit me. I tasted blood from where my lip had split. Daddy yelled that now he would have to "fix the problem."

My baby, who held the promise of something pure to love, was not a problem to be fixed. I had a deep-seated fear inside me that this would not turn out well.

A New Place

As time and money permitted, Gene and I were able to move out on our own. As exciting as it should have been was as scary as it was. Although Earl had since been put back in prison, word traveled fast in our small town that he had now been released, filling my days and nights with terror.

Gene was still working an unbelievable number of hours, often leaving me home alone. Waves of fear would hit me at all times of the day. I couldn't sleep at night without Gene beside me; even when he was there, I had constant flashbacks of the tapping on the window as Earl beckoned me to the cellar.

Being outside brought additional fear. Every time I heard the crunching of gravel from a car passing by or saw an old station wagon, memories would flare up, immediately taking my thoughts back to the shack.

The constant berating of my mind made my days unbearable. The bitterness in me continued to grow as everything in and around me constantly attacked my psyche. Everyone else seemed to walk through life happily; I couldn't help but wonder why I was getting meaner and angrier with each passing day.

My fears and stifled emotions began to seep out, which were justified as Earl soon invaded my life again. He had an uncanny ability to locate me, always able to find my phone number and where I lived. When he called, I would slam down the phone, shaking and angrily cussing. One time he came to my front door, but thankfully it was locked, and he could not get in. Still, my heart stopped when I saw his all-too-familiar figure through the window, terrorizing me again. Then something new washed over me. I realized that now I had the control; I could hide from him. So I crouched behind my furniture.

Hiding from anything that came against me became a new form of protection.

Gene hated my father, and it hurt him deeply that I lived in such fear. Because I was alone so often, he bought me a German Shepherd for companionship and protection. We named him Derrick. He was always with me—his presence was comforting and gave me a sense of security.

Eventually, Gene and I both realized I needed to go to work to help make ends meet. But finding a job was no easy task, as my social and cognitive skills were sorely lacking. Besides not understanding the basics of a workplace, I had an issue with severely distrusting people. I immediately thought the worst of others, and with no filter, my mistrust became crippling.

As my frustration grew, it continued to show up in the form of coarse language. My default of swearing was a defense mechanism brought on by years of abuse and exacerbated by how I saw the world. So, I went from job to job. As you can imagine, my regular outbursts did not fit in with a professional atmosphere.

Gene begged me over and over to please control my mouth, but I never saw the point. Often, he would lay a Bible on me as I slept, hoping that it would miraculously change me. But all that did was intensify my anger. Now, as I look back, it breaks my heart to recognize how my patient husband tried so hard to break through my tough exterior. Despite knowing the intricacies of my past and witnessing my current behavior, Gene was somehow always able to be there for me—without judgment.

We continued to hobble through life for the upcoming years. Me, with my chosen barriers, which continued to isolate me, and Gene, with his ever-present kindness and patience.

Then, a miracle occurred. I got pregnant again. Thoughts of losing the baby haunted me continually. But to our joy and surprise, our son Brent was born. He was healthy, and I adapted to motherhood. Our second son, Brad, was born four years later, completing our precious family.

Although I loved being a mother, I had no idea the extent to which those boys would change my life.

Jocinda

Jocinda bent over in her chair. She put her face in her hands and listened as the lady talked about having a son. Two sons. She breathed into her hands and felt the warmth of her breath. Her mind went back to that cold morning when she walked down the street with her daddy as her baby grew inside her. Jocinda's hands had been freezing, even though they were in her pockets. She had hoped her baby wasn't cold.

Daddy woke me up early and told me to get dressed. I didn't know where we were going, but I knew not to make him wait. It had only been a few days since Queenie said I was pregnant, and daddy had reacted badly. He really hadn't even talked to me since. I didn't know how he was going to "fix the problem." All kinds of thoughts rolled around in my head.

When we got to the clinic, it was the first time I ever heard the word "abortion." The nurse explained what they were going to do, but I didn't understand. All I knew was that they were going to "take care of things for me."

What they did to me was unlike anything I even knew existed. It was so quick. It took longer for us to walk there than it did for them to "fix my problem." They finished and took me to the recovery area.

The nurse walked away, and I was alone. There was no one to care for me.

There was no baby, no happiness, and no life.

I was empty.

Walking through Agony

As the boys grew and our lives progressed, we eventually moved to a new small town.

Brent and Brad ventured out and met the twin boys who lived directly across the street. They were involved in sports together, and their friendship grew. The twins' mother often drove the foursome to practice and periodically had my sons over to play. This went on for years. Despite their friendship, I kept my barriers raised. Not caring to know anyone, I stayed to myself, living in my own isolated world.

One day, as I was walking through the neighborhood, the twins' mother, whose name I learned was Marilyn, saw me outside as she drove by. She rolled down the window to introduce herself and ask me how my day was. She proceeded to tell me that she and her husband enjoyed having the kids around to play with her boys. She tried to be friendly, asking me more questions, but with my lack of social skills, I felt like she was nosey and battering me.

"I don't see you very often. Do you work?"

Maybe if I ignore her, she'll go away.

"Do you go to church?"

Why was that her business?

"Would you like to come over for coffee?"

Who does she think she is?

I wasn't interested in answering her questions or meeting her for coffee. The only person I was comfortable talking with besides my immediate family was Gene's mother, and I certainly didn't want to have any sort of conversation with my nosey neighbor—no matter how much my kids liked her.

That first interaction with Marilyn started a rhythm that was almost comedic.

Marilyn would knock on my door; I would hide.

Marilyn would approach me; I would walk the other way.

Marilyn would send invitations through the boys; I would not respond.

Despite my aversion to wanting anything to do with my neighbor, it was easy and convenient to allow her to take my boys places they wanted to go. Of course, they loved sports, so she was always taking them to their little league games. Gene would show up when he could, but I rarely went.

The only thing I did regularly was my work at the factory. It was a job, not exciting, but one I had finally been able to hold. Every day, I stood in an assembly line. My co-workers and I were just an arm's length apart. We weren't supposed to talk to each other as we worked, which was just fine with me. We each focused on the routine of accurately filling our quota. The machinery was so loud and repetitive that it would have been impossible to hear each other anyway.

Far and above the sound of the machinery was the barrage of thoughts that relentlessly pounded in my brain. The voices in my head grew louder and louder, tormenting me. They made me wonder why I even existed. Unwelcome thoughts resounded, telling me that there was no purpose in my existence, so maybe I should just take control of the situation and end my own life. Planning scenarios for my death allowed me to drown out the voices and the repetitive nature of my job.

With no drive, both work and home became monotonous. At home, I would stare out the window and catch glimpses of Marilyn and her husband. I couldn't understand why they were so happy. Seeing her run out to greet her husband with a kiss when he arrived home was so foreign to me. I watched them leave for church each Sunday with their Bibles in hand. Their smiles and laughter were full of light, which perplexed me as to why my own life was heavy and dark.

I had limited interaction with Marilyn and her husband, but they never quit pestering me. They were always kind and peaceful, playing gospel music in their cars and inviting me to church. Sometimes, they made an appearance at our drinking parties, but they never consumed any alcohol. Their joyful demeanor remained consistent, catching my attention. She was always telling me about God—making sure I knew I could talk to Him directly, which made me roll my eyes as I schemed how to get away from her. This went on for quite some time.

Marilyn and her family's regular church attendance eventually influenced Brent and Brad. The boys told Gene and me they wanted to go to church, too; although I agreed they could go, I wanted no part of it myself. The mere thought of the whole Sunday routine triggered memories of my time at the children's home. Going to church itself was never so bad, but what happened to me afterward was intricately connected in my mind. Returning to the home, dressed in my Sunday best, I was often raped by Earl, who had access to me during his visitation. My view of church was tarnished, and I just couldn't allow that old wound to be opened. So, I permitted the boys to go with Marilyn and her family, only perpetuating my isolation and loneliness.

One day, the boys excitedly invited me to go to a "tent meeting." I didn't know what a tent meeting was, but they said it would be fun. Because of their enthusiasm, I agreed to go with them, not understanding what I was getting into.

When we arrived at the open field, there was guitar music and people singing. Everyone around seemed happy—like Marilyn. But something about being there began to scare me. I endured the event for a while, but I couldn't wait for it to be over.

Finally, wanting to escape the scene, I made my way back to the car and sat alone, waiting for the kids to return. Suddenly, Brad and Chris, one of Marilyn's sons, came running to the car. Breathing heavily and with looks of awe on their faces, words poured out of their mouths as they tried to explain that they had seen an intensely bright light in the cow field and were flabbergasted when they realized it was an angel.

With escalating fear, I told them to get in the car immediately. Then I remembered Marilyn's words, telling me I could speak directly to God. Immediately, I unashamedly pleaded with Him, "God, if you get me out of here, I will never go back to anything like this again."

I did get out of there. The fear I had felt and the promise I made bolstered my guard against Marilyn as she continued to pursue me. Her pestering intensified, so I always made sure to lock my front door and often pretended I wasn't home.

That was when Marilyn's words began reaching me from inside my own home as my boys began to speak about God.

Brent and Brad often arrived home from church, telling me, "Mom, you need to be born again."

I didn't even know what that meant.

They would continue, "Invite Jesus into your heart. The church is praying for you."

I angrily replied, "Why would they be praying for me?" I couldn't imagine what those people wanted from me.

Brent and Brad would respond, "Because without Jesus, you will die and go to hell."

I was plenty scared, and I didn't understand those words. Beyond being frightened of what I didn't know, I was also mad. My boys' attempts at persuasion were ongoing. However, the thoughts of ending my life continued to invade my mind, drowning out everything the boys and Marilyn would say.

One Sunday, as I sat drinking a lot of beer, I envisioned different ways how to kill myself. The demanding voices permeated my head, telling me over and over again to take my life. Trying to escape the madness, I finally got up and went to the store. When I returned home, I heard someone crying. Following the sound to the garage, my boys were inside a cardboard box where they regularly played. They were praying to Jesus, saying, "Save our mother."

This infuriated me. I went over to the box and kicked it as hard as I could. "I've had enough of this! Don't you pray for me! Get out of this garage now!"

I turned, fuming, and stormed back into the house. Then I heard crying again, coming from another room. I got up to see what was going on. It was Brent, bawling. As a mother, my heart should have broken for him. But I was filled with evil. And I was mean.

I was running from God.

I told the boys I didn't want them ever talking to me about God again or discussing me at church. I didn't want them or anyone else "praying for me."

This began a more intense period of hiding. I began hiding not only from Marilyn but also from everyone else: the church, the townspeople, and especially God.

Jocinda

God? Hiding from God? That's a laugh.

Jocinda smirked.

I've seen a parade of preachers come through the prison during my time here. I'm well aware of the annoying empty words people say about God.

They all talk about how much God loves us and wants the best for us. Well, if He loved us, why would He put us in here? So much for God's love and eternal salvation.

Some of the preachers she'd seen wore robes; others looked like the ones on TV who would cry at the drop of a hat. But it didn't matter what they wore. Jocinda didn't believe any of them. She didn't know if God even existed. She knew the only thing she could rely on was herself. She was alone.

Anyway, if there is a God, He couldn't even begin to love me after all I've done. I wouldn't have to hide from Him; He'd run from me.

The more she thought about God and how this lady was "hiding from Him," the angrier Jocinda became.

God has never been there for me.

Drawn into Darkness

I succeeded at being alone, but my drinking and self-deprecating thoughts escalated. Finally, Marilyn's persistence wore me down, and in a weak moment, I agreed to attend a local football game with her. While we were at the game, Marilyn's kindness broke through the exterior of my defenses. She gently asked me if I needed prayer, saying, "I know nothing about you, Dana."

The voice in my head shouted, "Of course, she doesn't know about you. Why would she? You are unlearned, unclean, and unimportant." Still, somehow, I began to share little bits about myself with her.

The words I verbalized prompted her to say, "The power of wrong thinking has taken over your mind."

As I opened up a little more, Marilyn continued with grace, "Since your childhood, Dana, you've had all the wrong feelings about yourself."

Then, she began telling me that Jesus could heal my heart.

I didn't shut her out.

The next day, even as I was still processing our conversation, I went to work at the factory. There, I received the devastating news that I was going to be let go from my job due to my constant filthy language. I ran to the bathroom and looked in the mirror. As I did, those demonic voices began screaming in my head again. Full of degrading and vile accusations, they now manifested themselves into something nearly tangible on my shoulder.

"Go jump in the lake!" they commanded, knowing I couldn't swim.

And then I heard them shout with boldness, "Run into traffic!"

I knew if I listened, I would be gone in an instant. *But wouldn't that be easier anyway?*

The voices had me under their control.

I looked in the mirror and saw an unfamiliar face. The reflection looked crazy and wild. At that moment, I was scared of myself.

I instantly decided to respond obediently, following the pattern of all the demands put on me in my past. As thoughts of Earl, the lawyers, and the housemother raced through my mind, I surrendered to the mandate from the voices to end my life.

Startled, I was suddenly called back to the assembly line to finish my shift. Loud machines roared in the background while the even louder voices continued tormenting me with their constant barrage of commands. My body kept methodically working while my mind spiraled into crazed confusion.

This was it. Wanting to silence the cacophony in my head and rid the world of my useless self, I planned to go home and put an end to it all.

Jocinda

Jocinda locked eyes with the lady again.

Their stories were alike in so many ways, and this was yet another. They shared a hopelessness that demanded they end it all. Jocinda had heard the same demonic voices. They came to her at night when everything was quiet. Prison can be deathly quiet. She could hear them telling her she was worthless, dirty, and forgotten. She, too, had thought about ways to end it all.

She could pick a fight with someone she knew could kill her either with their bare hands or a shiv, one of those homemade knives that so many inmates had.

She could try to escape, and maybe the guards would shoot her and put her out of her misery.

The easiest would be to hang herself. She had even timed the rounds the guards made to see if she had enough time to loop a bedsheet noose over the ceiling joist and end it all.

But she never did. At least not yet.

I've wanted to die. I have done so many things that I often think the best thing that could happen to me would be death. Life is cheap in here. People die all the time. Even if you don't stop breathing, your spirit dies. That's the worst. You just stop feeling.

Preparing to Die

When I got home from my last shift, Gene and the boys were out at a sporting event for the day with Marilyn's husband and the twins. I began working with purpose. Obsessing about the cleanliness of my home, I scrubbed every inch with extra vigor. I had always been a clean freak, but now I was working toward a goal. My minutes left on this earth were few, and I didn't want to leave any trace of the unclean aura that ruled my life.

Finishing with the housework, I set the scene for my death. I gathered as many pills as I could find and put them on my nightstand. The more pills, the better; I wanted to die quickly. I even found a red bedspread and laid it on my bed. I had never done this before, and I didn't know if, in the end, blood would seep out my nose or ears or from anywhere else. And I didn't want my bed to be ruined or to leave a big mess.

Making my way back to the kitchen, I evaluated my cleaning efforts. When I was satisfied that everything was okay and in order, I started back down the hallway, ready to go to my bedroom and take my life.

Suddenly, the phone rang, catching me off guard. Without taking time to think, I answered it. It was Marilyn.

"Dana, I called to tell you something."

"Yeah?"

Crying, Marilyn said, "Jesus loves you. Jesus LOVES YOU!"

"Okay."

Marilyn kept crying. I hung up.

Resuming my plan, I went down the hallway to the bedroom, determined to die. I was so excited! I was the saddest excuse for a person.

JESUS loves me? I couldn't even fathom the thought. I knew I was loved by Gene, the boys, and even his family, but I had yet to understand the full meaning of love. I didn't know that love is the foundation of life and provides meaning and purpose. I couldn't comprehend that an incomprehensible force was trying to break through my barriers of pain, anger, and self-destructive desires.

I was teeming with bitterness and hate. I despised my life. I was trapped in an existence of being unclean, unimportant, and unlearned. The voices in my head were all-consuming. I knew I could never get away from them. Even when Gene held me tight in his arms so I could go to sleep, horrific dreams tormented me. There was simply no relief in my existence.

Taking my life was my only option to find relief.

Jocinda

Wait a minute. If she was so determined to kill herself, why is she here? Why is this woman who has been through so much, including wanting to kill herself, here?

Jocinda smirked. *Maybe she just wasn't very good at anything. Even ending her own life.*

Stepping into My Destiny

I made my way back down the hallway to my room. Approaching the bedroom, I turned the handle and opened the door.

I entered and prepared to die.

Jocinda

J ocinda sat up. She had been listening to the woman speak and hearing the words, but now something told her that she HAD to listen. Almost as if an unseen force was pulling her into the woman's story.

Her mind was clear. She listened as if her own life depended on the next words that would be spoken.

Touched

I stepped into my bedroom and was suddenly taken aback by the powerful yet gentle touch of a hand on my left shoulder. Instantly, a sea of warmth engulfed me. In that moment of stillness, the unexpected sensation calmed and soothed me as the room inexplicably lit up with the brightest and most astonishing light I had ever seen.

Or maybe I had seen it before. Once. That night in the children's home.

The night the angel had visited me.

Then I heard voices. Lots of voices. These were different—not the individual gruff voices that had tormented me for so long, but a glorious melody full of beautiful harmonies—like the most exquisite choir I had ever heard. The heavenly singing penetrated my soul as I felt a peace and assurance I had only felt that one time when I had seen the angel.

I had forgotten that feeling existed.

And I began to cry.

I never cried—not in private or around anyone. I was told not to cry. I, Dana Louise Cryer, was not allowed to cry. Besides, I had learned so many years before that crying would never do me any good. So I never cried around Gene, or my kids, or anybody. I learned to hold it in and had instead become cold and bitter. I had no compassion for anyone or anything. Even myself.

But now, tears of cleansing fell unashamedly down my face.

My intense sobbing depleted me, making me weak and unstable. Walking toward my bed, I found it difficult to stay upright due to the heaving of my body. Then, despite extreme frailty, my arms were instantly infused with strength as they were propelled upward, extending high above my head. My body couldn't help but involuntarily praise God. As if that wasn't enough, a language came out of my mouth that I could not understand. I somehow knew I was speaking words of love and adoration for our heavenly Father. In my utter weakness, I felt an exuberant strength I had never experienced before.

I was entirely unaware that Gene and the boys had returned home. They were in the living room with Marilyn, who had come over, responding to an undeniable internal urge to be present and available. Somehow knowing this was a pivotal moment in my life, they were praying with intensity. Hearing me crying and crying, Gene and the boys ached to intervene. But speaking with authority and love, Marilyn assured them that the best thing they could do for me was to remain on their knees in prayer. She told them over and over again, "God has Dana."

Still inside my bedroom with the door shut, I remembered what Brent and Brad had told me. "Mom, you have to ask Jesus into your heart. Ask Him to forgive your sins so you won't go to hell."

Their prayers and my inexplicable encounter went on for two hours.

Reflection fell upon me as I vividly replayed every aspect of my life. Incredibly intense emotions took over my whole being as torment and torture radiated to my very bones. I saw the little girl I had been—abused and forgotten. And I finally recognized that my whole callous attitude about life and people had come from my pain and anger. I had never let anyone in. I distrusted everyone and saw the bad in them and myself. I had let myself become full of hate and bitterness.

Confusion consumed me as questions ran through my head.

Is the rage I live with justifiable? Can I possibly let go of it?

Did the abuse inflicted on me in my childhood cause wounds that changed who I am forever?

Has darkness and coldness become the true center of my being? Or is there something else within me?

What did I do wrong to deserve all I've gone through? Is this all my fault?

I simply couldn't understand my own behavior or how I had gotten to where I was.

I continued to sob while my thoughts spun in circles, trying to make sense of the turbulence in my soul. I was seeking clarity. The truth was that so much had been done TO me. And right or wrong, it was my story. But as certainly as I understood this, I also knew beyond the shadow of a doubt that my story wasn't over. I was in the middle of my story. Not at the end. God had more for me.

I finally grasped the meaning of those previously elusive words the angel spoke to me so many years earlier at the children's home.

"Jesus loves you."

Jesus loves me!

This wasn't new information, but I had never before recognized the truth contained within those three words.

I could now see clearly beyond the words.

God's love had flowed into every aspect of my life through His abundant care and provision. Despite years of neglect, I had survived.

Through horrific abuse, **GOD ALONE WAS ABLE** to equip me with endurance and strength beyond all human realization. Every day of my life, He was there protecting me with His strong arm, even sending His angels at my darkest moments.

In the true manner of His essence, He lavishly provided me with a God-fearing man and a new mother, Gene's mother, who accepted me as her own.

Then God overcame my tattered and torn womb, blessing me with adoring and forgiving sons who had a deep faith I couldn't begin to understand.

With triumphant tears, I understood for the first time that Marilyn's presence in my life was yet another gift from God. I wouldn't respond to Him, so He had sent Marilyn to me. With her relentless love and never-ending patience and care, she never allowed my rejection of her to deter her God-given mission. In her obedience, she embodied the joy God intends for each of us.

God knows exactly who He created me to be, and He has never stopped pursuing me.

Despite what I had been through and even who I had become in response to my pain and anger, God showed me that I am not defined by my circumstances or what others inflict on me.

The definition of who I am is determined solely by God.

I am Dana Louise Cryer.

GOD LOVES ME.

My story is His story. And my story is far bigger than abuse or pain or neglect.

As the hours passed, I continued to cry out to God through my tears, processing His faithfulness to me. Even though I was bruised with inequity, God's overwhelming love for me had continually shined through the cracks of my life.

I clearly recounted each painful episode of my life, but now the beams of light that pierced the darkness were outshining all the pain, anger, and hurt I had endured.

More than anything else, I now recognized the radiating goodness of God that flowed through my tattered walls—the barriers that encompassed my life. God's beams of light that had illuminated each trial I endured.

Although I had been discarded by my parents, Uncle Howard and Aunt Mildred grounded me with their unconditional love. When I was isolated in the shack, I was never alone. The Holy Spirit had calmed my soul through the sound of the wind. The train whistle, the manifestation of God's soothing power, had brought me hope and comfort. Even the beautiful kitty who delivered me a brief but so impactful moment of joy and tenderness was created by God for ME.

I reflected with joy, recalling the happiness God had allowed me to have as I grew and learned from my half-brothers and Helen, playfully frolicking with them in the sunshine. I could now see that those moments of my carefree existence overcame the darkness of my cellar imprisonment.

Even though I didn't recognize God's actions or His presence, it was suddenly clear that, all along, He had been infusing me with His strength and enabling me to stand in His power despite all that should have destroyed me.

In another miraculous turn, God had provided me with Helen's secure presence as we were whisked away to the children's home, fraught with uncertainties. I remembered, with clarity, the one teacher at school who had spoken life into my very existence. I had never seen that teacher again, but his actions were a beam of light from God, creating indelible impressions on my heart that would last for eternity.

And then, when all seemed lost yet again, God sent the angel who told me directly of Jesus' love for me.

God had been there all along. I just never knew it. He was holding me, guiding me, and comforting me.

God had been so good to me. *Is this love?*

I was hit with the reality of every aspect of my life. I cried tears of repentance as I saw how I had become so callous, never letting anyone in. My heart had hardened as I built a barrier that nothing could pierce.

Nothing but the unrelenting love of God.

God was able to crack that wall I had so carefully constructed. He broke through it with His love and light of mercy and grace. Though I was centered on pain and steadfast immovability, He had brought me out—from confusion to clarity.

I am His. And that is enough.

Then, I remembered my precious boys' words again.

"Mom, you need to be born again. Invite Jesus into your heart. Without Jesus, you will die and go to hell."

Jocinda

Jocinda could barely breathe as she listened.

The entire room of about 75 women was silent. You could have heard a pin drop. Every person was hanging on every word.

If ANYONE else had said what this woman just said, I would have never believed it. But she is so genuine, so sincere, so honest. It has to be real.

Jocinda thought about the decisions she had made in her life.

I've done some bad things. Heck, I shot and killed my daddy. Hate and anger have filled every inch of me—it now runs in my blood.

God could never love me like He loves this woman. Of that, I am totally sure. I've done so many horrible things. It just isn't possible.

Still...

...

...

...

...her words are penetrating my brain.

And all those bad things that were done to HER...they make me think about the things that have been done to me.

How have I responded? Have I built my own walls?

Finding Relief in God's Arms

"You need to be born again."

That phrase rang through my mind as I released everything to God. I let go of all the strongholds in my life—the fear, the pain, the uncertainties. I gave them all to God, and a flood of peace entered my very being.

I confessed to God that I had not trusted Him. I had allowed all of the bitterness and anger and my own need for control to build in me, creating a barrier blocking me from His perfect love. In that miraculous moment, the fortress within me came crashing down into a pile of dust that God graciously swept away.

As I yielded to His strength and melted in His presence, I joyfully declared the words, "I am Yours!"

Instantly, I felt a relief I had never experienced before.

The pouring out of all that was in me cleansed my spirit as I replaced my staunch indignation with the recognition of Jesus as my Savior.

Without hesitation or self-consciousness, I put a name to each of the bricks I had used to build the insurmountable wall around my heart. And as I confessed each of my shortcomings, every brick crumbled into remnants that were whisked away by winds of God's forgiveness.

I exhaled in exuberance, recognizing that God had protected me from taking my life.

Although the enemy had been prodding me into self-destruction for so long, God stepped in at just the right moment. Just minutes before I was going to take the pills, His ever-present glory manifested itself in a form I could not deny.

The Holy Spirit knew exactly how to reach me, and, praise God, I was open to accepting His presence. He had been with me through my brokenness, and He had a plan to use all I had gone through. He had literally touched my shoulder as I was walking toward my death, overwhelming me with the warmth of His hand. With the warmth of His love.

I lifted my hands and cried as I experienced God from the top of my head to the soles of my feet; I shouted words of praise to God as I spoke in tongues. In a split second, I had been completely changed forever by God's love for me. He embraced me, and I've never wanted to turn back.

Still standing in my bedroom, I continued to cry. It was so simple and easy. God tenderly caught my tears with His love, exchanging my bitterness for His joy. He allowed my heart to understand the meaning of the word love. Finally.

Although I had never forgotten the words from the angel, "Jesus loves you," they had perplexed me all these years. But now, I was filled with God's unconditional acceptance of who I am. I experienced this gift of His love, which gives us the greatest freedom to let go of whatever attempts to steal our peace and joy.

In that moment, I learned a valuable, life-changing lesson: God gives us the freedom to run into His arms no matter what we have been through. He does not hold anything over us or against us. His love moves us forward into the miraculous future He has planned for each of us.

I looked out into the faces of the inmates, continuing to share my life story. I wanted them to understand that this was the most important transformation anyone could ever experience. We are all called to a life of freedom and abundance. We are all created to be God's children. He never leaves us alone in this world. He is always walking with us and calling us to stand in His presence.

The power behind my words grew.

I, Dana Louise Cryer, had merely existed in a shack, yet God had already designed so much more for my future. He freed me so He could use my pain for His purpose—to share His love with everyone who would listen.

That small bedroom where I wanted to end my life had been transformed by transcending love. Though I planned for it to become my tomb of death, God was able to make it a place of rebirth for my life. I lay across the bed for several hours, basking in the presence of the Holy Spirit. My whole body tingled with joy and the expectation of all God had in store for me. I knew my life was just beginning.

Gene, the boys, and Marilyn finally came into the room and asked if I was okay.

I answered, "I am now. I just asked Jesus into my heart."

Jocinda

Jocinda's head was reeling. What had started as a day to come to listen to some lady's story had become a moment of deep reflection.

Jocinda thought about all the times she had come to a crossroads in her life. The first moment she made the decision to steal. The first time she let herself give in to hate and how that had become her "normal."

And, of course, the first time Violet had come to visit her in prison. Jocinda told the guards she didn't want to see her because she didn't want to spoil any memories Violet might have of her. She didn't want Violet to see how far she had fallen.

And the other times that Violet had tried to connect with her—the letters, phone calls, and visits. Every time, Jocinda had chosen to ignore the attempts.

"Transformed by transcending love." That's what the woman said. I don't even know what that is. How do you get it? How can someone like me go from where I am today to where she is in her heart? It's not possible.

As the lady continued to speak, Jocinda saw the years of hate and fear fall away from the woman. It was as if she was transforming before Jocinda's eyes. She could see it, but she didn't understand it. There was just "something" there.

Going Forward

As the sun shined through my bedroom window the morning after my miraculous transformation, the glow within me remained as brilliant as it had been the day before. I asked Gene to bring me the Bible he had given me years earlier. He gently honored me by laying it on my lap without chastisement. He never brought up the belligerent attitude I had always exhibited toward the Bible.

Through his actions, I recognized that Gene had always been the epitome of forgiveness and unconditional love in our relationship. The husband that God had gifted me with was a picture of His own grace and mercy. God had always been leading me to life, not death. Now, I was drawn by an insatiable quest to understand Him and His Word.

As I sat with the Bible on my lap, it fell open to a verse, Psalm 27:10. Although I still had problems with literacy, miraculously, I was able to read and understand the powerful words of this verse: *When my father and my mother forsake me, then the Lord will take me up* (Psalm 27:10 KJV).

At that moment, I completely understood that God had adopted me as His own daughter. He loved me with abandon. I marveled as I grasped that anything the enemy had taken from me would be given back in abundance. Joy filled my soul.

My hands shook, and I fell to my knees with my head down in reverence for my great and mighty Comforter. I stayed in that position for an indefinable amount of time as God strengthened me by pouring His love into my tattered heart. He spoke to me, telling me He would always walk with me. My love for Him and my desire to read the Bible grew from that moment forward.

The Holy Spirit sparked another flame within me—an eagerness to attend church. I simply couldn't wait for the next service. I called Marilyn and, for the first time, asked her if I could accompany her. This thrilled her! My own excitement escalated when we walked into the church to find everyone celebrating. I was overcome when I was told the reason for the jubilance: They were rejoicing over my salvation. They even had a water baptism ready for me.

I met many wonderful people that day, including a loving pastor and his wife, Susie. They welcomed me into my new family, taking me in with open arms of acceptance. Susie and I connected right away. We began a powerful friendship; she called me often to pray with me and guide me on this new journey.

During these precious days of my new beginning, I began having distinct dreams and visions.

In my first impactful dream, I was walking in a different realm. I progressed down a pathway and could see a mansion ahead in the distance. As I approached it, I saw many empty rocking chairs lined up on the front porch. In the last chair on the right, there was a man I was drawn to. I walked closer and recognized that it was Jesus. He was rocking, with His head bowed toward something He was tenderly holding in His arms. I heard someone talking but couldn't make out what they were saying. Then, as I got closer, I recognized the voice—it was my Jesus. He was whispering softly to a baby He was cradling.

Everything suddenly became still as the baby's head turned toward me, showing me her face. I was overcome with emotion as God revealed that the object of Jesus' love and attention was Baby Dana. Swaddled in His arms, I was resting, protected and loved as He rocked and comforted me with His words.

The sight was beautiful as I watched from the path, smiling so big with unrestrained tears falling from my eyes. I processed with wonder and awe that Jesus had been holding and comforting me all the days of my life.

Two nights later, I had another dream. In this dream, I was at home, and many people were arriving at my door. Each person rolled up their pant legs before coming in because there was knee-deep water throughout the house. Together, we sloshed around in the refreshing water with laughter and happiness.

The next day, I called Susie and told her about the dream. She said the water signified the Holy Spirit's presence in my home. He had filled my life with springs of living water, cleansing and healing me and allowing me to share His refreshment with everyone around me.

Susie also foretold that God had given me the gift of prophecy. She explained that my dreams had meaning and significance, and I was to share them with others. She also proclaimed I would be speaking to the world and telling everyone of the joy of Jesus, using my story as a vehicle. Susie prayed over me, asking God to help me with my mind. She prayed that I would remember and share details of my life so others could see the glory of God, who alone was able to save and complete me. Susie assured me that this word was from Jesus.

I learned from Susie that one of the ways God grows us is to make us aware of all He is doing in our lives. For this reason, she helped me journal about the many miraculous events that were unfolding. As we processed together, God's hand on my entire life became clear.

I often woke up in the middle of the night, knowing God wanted to tell me something. At first, He repeated to me, "Eyes and ears. Eyes and ears."

Not understanding the message but unable to ignore it, I got out of bed and went to the living room. When I turned on the light and opened the Bible, God's message to me was illuminated when I read 1 Corinthians 2:9, *But as it is written,*

Eye hath not seen, nor ear heard, neither have entered into the heart of man, the things which God hath prepared for them that love him (KJV).

Though I still had a difficult time understanding anything I read, God provided me with insightful knowledge of this scripture. I cried so much because I understood that the Bible is a love letter He wrote to me. And I knew beyond a shadow of a doubt that God wanted me to enhance my reading skills so I could further understand His Word and discover who I was as a Christian. The King James Bible my husband had bought me years earlier became my ever-constant companion. I started reading it nonstop. I had an insatiable hunger for the Word of God.

I thought all Christians experienced this same longing in their lives. I was so happy and excited and just wanted to run and tell everyone what I was seeing, reading, and dreaming. But I quickly became surprised that not everyone wanted to hear it.

In our journaling sessions, I told Susie about the many ways God had been speaking to me, and I was encouraged by her joyful response to everything I shared. She continued to mentor me as I bloomed from the darkness into God's ever-present light. She once again prophesied over me, proclaiming I would speak in front of thousands, be on television, and even write a book about my life. All to glorify God. Now, I can say that her prophecy was truly from God—all of these things have come to be. What God ordains, no one can come against.

My public journey began quite unexpectedly one day at church when a guest speaker called me forward. He was praying and laying hands on people and wanted to speak over me. As I stood before the whole congregation, he told me that I had the gift of love.

Taken aback, I said, "What?" Only recently had I even begun to understand what love was. How could this be my gift?

He then said, "I've never seen this before. Dana Louise, you are gifted with a spirit of love."

God proceeded to touch my heart as He filled me from my head to my toes with His love. Despite being dumbfounded, I still could not comprehend what a great gift this was. Having now lived many years, I can vow that love was indeed the gift God wanted me to have all along. I've since learned to embrace it with God's power.

But before I could truly love, I needed to forgive. That would be a process for me.

Jocinda

Jocinda thought about the many preachers who had come to the prison and passed out Bibles. Some Bibles were the little ones that fit in your pocket, and others were the bigger ones with the Thee's and Thou's. Usually, she had declined the offer, but sometimes, the people who brought them were persistent. They would practically throw a Bible at you.

She had started to read one a few times—more out of boredom than anything else. But most of the time, if she did take one, it wouldn't make it past the first trash can she came to.

Now, Jocinda wondered, *Was I missing something?*

Learning to Forgive

My world changed yet again when Marilyn moved. But this, too, was orchestrated by God as He brought me a new neighbor and lifelong friend. Nancy moved into the house across the street where Marilyn had lived. Even with my simplistic newfound faith, I understood this was not an accident. I became determined to meet Nancy.

She and her family had started going to the same church I was attending, but our first meeting was not overly friendly. One of Nancy's daughters told me her mother thought I was weird. Still, I pressed harder to get to know her. Much like Marilyn's pursuit of me early on, I captivated Nancy with love by joyfully sharing how great God is and all the incredible things He was doing. I could not contain my excitement. And although, at first, Nancy tried to avoid me, neither of us could escape God's will for our friendship.

And so it was that one day, when Nancy and her husband were returning from a shopping trip at the local mall, she said to her husband, "I have to go to Dana's house." Then she called me, saying she was "supposed to" come by.

As Nancy entered my home, she quickly explained that she did not know why she was there but that I had to pray for her. She revealed that she just wanted to know if God was real and if all the great things I had been telling her were the truth. Exclaiming that they were, I laid hands on Nancy and prayed with her.

As time went by, Nancy and I leaned on each other as we learned of God's deeper teachings together. We upheld one another as sisters should, studying and growing and never losing enthusiasm to find the truth in God's Word. What a miracle it was to realize and come to believe that everything in the Bible was written specifically for us. Nancy and I were enveloped with a childlike faith as transcending truths permeated our thoughts. With thankful hearts, we studied the Bible and prayed together for hours.

Through these encounters, God continually showed me scriptures about forgiveness. The Holy Spirit was igniting a passion in me that became my new focus. I learned that in the Bible, God commands us to forgive those who have wronged us. I began to grieve deeply as I recognized my father's misconduct, wondering if God was asking me to forgive Earl for the years of pain and abuse.

As I questioned God about this, Marilyn, Nancy, and Susie were instrumental in helping me formulate my thoughts. I still couldn't write well, so they took it upon themselves to record in a journal all God was showing me. Our collaborative efforts—me processing God's direction and them transcribing all I was hearing—provided me with a precious blueprint to go forward with the plan God was revealing to me.

Although I knew I could not pardon my father's abusive and ruinous behavior towards me, I was convicted to forgive him.

Holding onto unforgiveness was a treacherous weight. Over time, I realized this stronghold of pain had festered into horrific bitterness and resentment, leading me to uncontrollable anger. Earl had broken the law and served time; but wasn't I breaking God's law by not forgiving my tormentor? Wasn't I in my own prison, held captive by the unforgiveness in my spirit?

The Bible teaches us to throw off our old selves and put on a spirit of mercy, kindness, humility, gentleness, and patience (Colossians 3:12). I prayed that God would shower me with those attributes and allow me to shed the tough exterior that had encompassed my heart for years. As I prayed, God reminded me of Jesus' great act of forgiveness towards me. He showed me again and again how I had offended Him, yet He had always responded with HIS love and forgiveness.

LEARNING TO FORGIVE

After much struggle, I decided I needed to forgive Earl, my abuser.

Not long after I made that life-changing decision, God promptly gave me a vision and, through it, the strength to submit in obedience. I saw God holding my father in one of His arms and me in the other. God looked at Earl and said, "I forgive him." Then He looked at me with love and compassion, releasing me with His upholding approval, saying, "Now, you forgive him."

I fell on my face, and oh, such crying and travailing deep within me occurred as all the years of anger, pain, and hatred were released and replaced with forgiveness for my father. Tears cleansed me from all the things that resided deep in my heart as peace and light permeated every part of my soul.

Jocinda

Jocinda was dismayed.

Had this woman lost her mind? How could she even think about forgiving that man who stole her childhood, raped her, and kept her from her education?

I can understand the hurt and the hate, but not the forgiveness. That was a sign of weakness.

No man who would ever do to another human what this man had done to her deserved to be forgiven. He deserved hate, harm, pain, and death. That was the only thing a man like that deserved.

Demonstrating Forgiveness

One Wednesday night, I was with Gene and the boys in church, deep in thought. Suddenly, an usher tapped me on the shoulder and whispered to me that I had a phone call. He took me to the church office and handed me the phone. It was my half-sister, Helen. We hadn't seen each other in a while, but we had always remained in contact.

Her words stunned me. "Earl is in the hospital in serious distress. He had a massive heart attack."

The next thing I knew, she was handing him the phone.

It was all happening so fast. I had no time to collect the thoughts that raced through my mind about the man who played such a diabolical role in my life. Although I had forgiven him in my heart, as I heard his unmistakable voice on the other end of the line, weak and vulnerable, I knew God was giving me an opportunity to put my heart change into action.

"Hi, Dana Louise."

I had no immediate compassion. But the Holy Spirit took hold of me, pouring unexpected words from my mouth like a faucet. "I got born again. I don't know if you will understand what I'm saying, but I asked Jesus into my heart. I asked Him into my heart, and now I know I will always be with Jesus."

Words continued to flow as I told him all about my beautiful new life with God. Then the unthinkable happened—I was compelled to ask Earl to forgive me.

"I'm sure you don't know, but I hated you for what you did to my life. I have felt anger, bitterness, and resentment toward you for most of my existence. Will you forgive me for that? That was my sin. I hated you. I already asked Jesus for His forgiveness, and now I'm asking you."

I knew that in God's eyes, my own anger, hate, and unforgiveness were not any different from the incest and abuse my father had inflicted on me. And, sensing his death could be near, I felt compelled to break down all barriers between us while it was still possible.

As he listened on the phone, I heard Earl begin to sob and cry. Through his bawling, he said, "I forgive you."

As I had grown in my own faith, I had learned that without Jesus, we are all lost and separated from God eternally. I couldn't bear the thought of my father's eternal separation from God.

Knowing that his heart had now softened and God had opened a door, I boldly said, "We both have to forgive each other. I want to be your daughter in heaven. Can I say a prayer with you so I know you'll be in heaven with me? Tell Jesus you are a sinner and ask Him to come into your heart. We don't have to make this long because Jesus is listening right now."

With both our voices shaking, I led him in a prayer of salvation. Catching his breath, Earl finished with intense deliberation, "I am a sinner. Jesus, will You come into my heart?"

We could barely speak, overcome with uncontrollable crying. My father's newfound freedom released tears that streamed down our faces.

"I'm going to send you a Bible and the prayer we just prayed."

Then, in a moment I will never forget, my earthly father asked, "Dana Louise, will you forgive me?"

I cried so hard with pure joy. Only God! He was able to move through me, allowing me to voice the words, "Yes. I forgive you. I love you."

"I love you, Dana Louise."

"Daddy, I love you. And I'll see you again."

Helen took the phone back as my father repeated with waves of emotion, "I'm sorry. I'm so sorry."

I was wailing and wailing. I knew a miracle had happened. I had known that I needed to focus on forgiveness and release my hatred to God. And, with His help, I did.

People often ask me with perplexity how I could ever have forgiven my father, who had destroyed my childhood. How could I excuse such abuse, neglect, and ongoing pain intentionally inflicted on me by someone who was supposed to protect and love me? He had selfishly robbed me of so much. How could I pardon him?

My reply is always: Jesus Christ forgives each of us. And because He forgives me, I have to do the same for others. There is no argument or debate.

Forgiveness is one of the most liberating things a Christian can and must do. The Bible clearly teaches us to walk in love toward the people who abuse us, abandon us, or hurt us. Only by obeying God's Word and walking in Jesus' love are we able to walk in the freedom He intends for us.

The next day, true to my word, I sent Earl a Bible along with the prayer of salvation.

That same morning, Helen called crying. "Daddy's dead."

He was 58. I can honestly say I know I will see my earthly father in heaven. I have tremendous relief knowing that he is a forgiven child of God.

Jocinda

Jocinda slumped a bit. Her inner conversation continued.

I never gave my father a chance. I only thought of him as an animal...but there were some good memories I've tucked away. He brought me a stuffed animal once. And there was the time he took me to get ice cream.

But he hurt me so.

I never gave my father a chance. Maybe somewhere inside, he loved me. I will never know.

I shot him and took his life. Can't be undone now.

Testifying of God's Power

I continued to grow, learning to pray on a deeper level and enjoying the sweetness of having a church family. Gene, the boys, and I never missed service. I eagerly studied the Word in my downtime and took every opportunity to mature in my faith as I learned with others. Nancy and I spent hours around the kitchen table together, unable to get enough of Jesus.

Gene, with his ever-present precious smile, was my biggest supporter. He had always respected and loved me. He had always known that God had His hand on me. But now he saw God's love, joy, peace, patience, kindness, goodness, faithfulness, gentleness, and self-control blossoming in me. He had believed in me for so long, and now he clearly saw the fruits of the Holy Spirit growing within me.

Brent and Brad were also beside themselves with joy. They had prayed for me for so long, even as they experienced the pain and anger I had exhibited daily that always brought them fear and uncertainty. It was so evident to them that God had graciously elevated me to a newfound joy, balancing out my pendulum-swinging emotions, which had previously caused such turmoil in all our lives. Now, my cherished boys were proud of me and the role they had played in my salvation. They were acutely aware of the comfort invading my life as I came to love Jesus more and more each day.

A pivotal moment occurred unexpectedly one day while I was sitting in church, soaking in the pastor's teaching. Little did I know that God was about to begin to use me in a new and significant way.

The pastor was preaching on forgiveness and the importance of walking in freedom from bitterness, anger, and hatred. My heart resonated with everything he was saying.

Looking toward me, he said, "Dana is free. And her daddy is free." Then, he called me forward, asking me to share my testimony.

With complete confidence, I got up and walked forward, not knowing what a testimony was. I whispered to the pastor that I didn't understand.

He responded, "Just share from your heart. Tell them your story."

I took a deep breath and began. The Holy Spirit poured from my lips concise words illustrating my painful childhood, the anger that had crippled my life, and the release brought by the forgiveness from my father. I finished with the incredible confirmation of God's glory: how my forgiveness of Earl had catapulted him into a saving relationship with Jesus. I joyfully proclaimed how God had given me the strength to forgive my abuser, which inspired and enabled Earl to recognize and accept God's saving grace, stating, "God is the only One *who is able* to offer true freedom."

I couldn't even contemplate everything happening. I finished speaking and, looking out, saw everyone in tears. That's when I knew God had anointed me to share this story.

I stood on the altar, crying and crying tears of incomprehensible joy. I was FREE! I had publicly testified of the miracle God was able to do in my life and Earl's life. I was free to cry in Jesus, experiencing the release, relief, and joy of true forgiveness.

Shortly after this breakthrough, I began traveling all over the country, sharing God's story in my life. I spoke for organizations, at churches and events, and even to the media. The lights and cameras I often encountered reminded me of the horror of the days when I was first rescued. But now, those lights were no longer illuminating the recording of heinous acts of the devil. Instead, they were spotlighting redemption reels of God's glory. His purposes for my life were being realized. By sharing and testifying of His goodness and mercy through every avenue provided, I clearly understood that each piercing, painful moment I went through was redeemed by God for a glorious eternal purpose.

Word of my story made its way to the producers of *The 700 Club*, who contacted me and asked if I would be willing to be interviewed for this Christian news and worship program that aired daily on television. I agreed, bolstered by the Holy Spirit.

When the day came, I was prepped for my on-air appearance. I was a bit star-struck when I found out that Pat Robertson himself, the esteemed host of *The 700 Club*, would be interviewing me. However, my jitters quickly evaporated when I spoke with him. He had such a kind and open demeanor that I felt as if we had been friends for a long time. By the time the on-air interview took place, I was completely comfortable and simply shared my story. I was taken aback when Pat Robertson, the stalwart of faith and composure, began to cry as I spoke. In fact, he began to cry so hard that he had to hand the microphone to someone else to finish the interview. Bewildered but not shaken, I continued, knowing I needed to share all God had done. Near the end of the segment, Pat Robertson returned to the set and spoke into the camera, saying this true forgiveness story had impacted him more than any other.

Many people continued to reach out to me, offering me the opportunity to share my miracle story. My church even provided a driver who graciously escorted Gene and me to venues all over the country to speak.

Jocinda

*S*o this was how it turned for her. This is where the woman and me are different.

She gets to go on TV and talk to crowds of people. She even has someone to drive her around to so that she can tell her story—just like she is doing right now.

Meanwhile, I have no freedom from this hell I'm in. I am surrounded by prison walls where no one wants to hear my story because they all have their own. There are hundreds, maybe thousands of people like me in prison everywhere. We all did bad things. We hated people and tried to hurt people and ourselves. But we don't get to be famous and have people feel bad for us because of what we've gone through.

We are just losers. Trash.

This woman won the "I got raped, and now I'm famous lottery."

It seems this God of hers just takes care of some people. I'm sure He's too busy to help trash like me.

Fighting with Evil

Being secure in my newfound relationship with God and faithfully responding to my calling didn't mean I was done growing. Still, what I learned next took me off guard: Even when we obediently follow God, darkness can still come against us.

Sometimes, when I was asleep and Gene was not at home, I would feel a heavy rubber-like substance lying on me. The force would pin me down and hold my mouth shut. Terrified and unable to scream for help, I was held motionless. The pressure, heavy on my chest and body, exerted such power over me. Because nothing was ever visible, I discerned it had to be evil, directly from the pit of hell.

During these occurrences, which happened with increasing frequency when I took naps during the day, I called on God to help me.

"God, what do I do? I pray and resist, but this thing is still tormenting me."

"Cover it with my blood."

So I would repeat again and again, "Jesus! Cleanse me with your blood," remembering that Jesus' blood is always available to us.

The Bible teaches us that life is in the blood. In the Old Testament, when the angel of death came to kill the firstborn of each family, God commanded the Israelites to cover their doorposts with the blood of an innocent lamb, telling them that it would protect the lives of the children. Then, the New Testament explains that when Jesus came to earth, He became a sacrifice for each of us. His blood was pure, unaffected by sin. When He was killed, His perfect blood was poured out, washing our sin and death away. Jesus' perfect blood conquers any evil, so I understood that claiming His blood over this situation was the answer.

As I cried out, "Jesus! Cleanse me with your blood," the evil force had no choice but to flee.

After each episode, my energy was completely drained. My whole body felt the same torment and bondage it had those thousands of times I lay in pain on that dirty mattress after Earl had sexually molested me.

At first, I never told anyone about these horrible encounters. I was too embarrassed and full of pride. I had come so far. It made no sense to me that now, as a Christian, I was being attacked by what was certainly an evil spirit.

Then, one day after church, I was speaking to some ladies and brought up this mysterious matter. To my shock, another lady said she had experienced the same thing!

My fellow prayer warriors and I began to pray that God would show me what this thing was and forever release me from its grip. We knew the power of using a name. God calls us each by the name He has given us, and it delights Him when we call Him by His names: Savior, Lord, Provider, Sustainer, Refuge, Healer, Comforter ... the list goes on because our God is immeasurable. I knew that this thing was so limited, and if I could call this enemy by its name, I would be able to exert the power of God upon it and banish it from my life forever.

Then, one day on television, the word "incubus" appeared on the screen in a commercial for shoes. I was so intrigued by this strange word; with my insatiable desire to continue learning, I looked it up in the dictionary. And what I found was astounding.

"Incubus" was described as an evil spirit that lies upon people in their sleep and has sexual intercourse with them. It oppresses the individual, giving a sense of heaviness and suffocation and awakening the sleeper, leaving a feeling of anxiety or terror like a nightmare.

A nightmare, indeed!

Wow! When I read that, I knew for certain that although God firmly had me in His grips as His child, Satan was still trying to harm me with the deception that he held the power over me.

The next time this invasive presence visited me, God showed His full control. Not only did I have the blood of Jesus, but I now knew the name of the spirit that was tormenting me, and God also sent in reinforcements. My faithful neighbor and sister in Christ, Nancy, called. Knowing something was wrong, she immediately came over. I told her about Incubus. Without hesitation, she anointed me with oil and rebuked this evil force.

Then we got our Bibles and began reading, trusting God's presence and wisdom in our great time of need. We were assured that God was our Helper as we read Luke 10:19, *Behold, I give unto you power to tread on serpents and scorpions, and over all the power of the enemy: and nothing shall by any means hurt you* (KJV), and then John 8:32, *And ye shall know the truth, and the truth shall make you free* (KJV).

We continued reading and praying in full faith, calling out on the blood of Jesus to eject the spirit of Incubus from my life permanently.

God won that battle. That evil spirit never returned.

Jocinda

"*The truth shall make you free.*"

I've heard that before, but I never knew it was in the Bible. Queenie had told me that Dr. Martin Luther King had said that same thing. Queenie talked about him a lot, about how he had done more for "our people" than anyone else. She said he was a powerful preacher and a "true man of God."

When I heard Queenie talk like that, I didn't know what it meant—for the truth to make you free. But I guess Dr. King was quoting the Bible, just like this woman.

Maybe she is a "true woman of God." If she is, what does that make me? Our lives have so much in common. Even that heaviness. I've never told anyone about that. I never thought anyone else went through something like that.

Jocinda got a chill as she thought about the heavy, dark feeling she had experienced.

It was different than the woman's inca-, inca-, ...whatever she called it. But it sounded so similar. It had to be related.

For nights on end, lying in her prison bed, Jocinda had felt the weight of shame and guilt about the decisions she had made in her life pressing down on her. She imagined the weight squeezing the life out of her.

If God won the battle against the evil spirit the woman was talking about, maybe He could do the same for me.

She sat up a bit straighter, determined to hear more. What this woman was saying was opening thoughts of hope Jocinda had abandoned many years before.

Maybe I should find one of those Bibles and see if it could help me.

Longing for a Mother

God continued to do amazing things as I moved forward in my life. My family and faith grew as I followed His call to share my story of forgiveness. And yet, there was still a missing piece of my heart. I was unaware God was already unfolding a miraculous plan that would enrich me further. He would soon fulfill the longing that had been growing within me to find my biological mother.

One particular Mother's Day, while I was in church, Brother Ferguson asked all the mothers and their children to come to the front for a time of celebration and prayer. I went forward with my boys, Brent and Brad, my heart full of joy and gratitude for my own path of motherhood.

But, as I looked around, a longing filled my spirit as I saw other families with multiple generations. There were women my age smiling down at their children even while they relished in the glow of their own mother's love and affection. Suddenly, I felt alone and orphaned as the need to know my own mom pressed on my heart stronger than it ever had.

I became distraught and felt intense pain from not being able to know the joy these women were experiencing. I couldn't help but feel sorrow as I thought about how my mother did not want me, had abandoned me, and then remained absent my entire life. There was a struggle that came from the unknown of never knowing why I had lived 37 years without her.

Thoughts circled in my mind: *Where is she? What is she like? Is my mother a good person?*

I was consumed with a desire for her to be near me on that Mother's Day as I silently cried out to God, "What about *my* mother? I would love to know who my mother is."

As I walked back to my seat, I clearly heard God's voice. "Go get the birth certificate. You'll find your mother."

At first, the thought confused me, but as I allowed my mind to process it, I remembered the puzzling envelope I had received five years earlier, right after Earl's death, addressed to Mrs. Dana Cryer. Inside was a torn birth certificate from Coconino County, Arizona, for "Unnamed Baby Girl," along with a notarized statement proclaiming the adoption of a child for a fee of $1.

Having no idea what this was or why it had been sent to me, I had absentmindedly shoved it into a drawer and forgotten about it.

After the service, we went to lunch. Despite the Mother's Day celebration, my thoughts could not move beyond this perplexing enigma. I clearly recalled my bewilderment upon opening that envelope so many years ago. And now, hearing God's words reverberate through my mind, I knew there must be a connection.

"Go get the birth certificate. You'll find your mother."

So when we got home, I immediately went searching. It had been years since I'd seen the envelope, and we had even moved during that period. *Did it get lost in the shuffle? Was it somewhere in a heap of trash? Or could it possibly be buried somewhere? In a box or in a drawer?* One thing was certain—it would be a miracle to find it now.

I opened a drawer. Nestled behind random papers and miscellaneous junk was the sought-after envelope. With shaking hands, I opened it and examined its contents. Clarity came over me—this was the miracle puzzle piece God told me to find. *I* was the "Unnamed Baby Girl." I had been born in Coconino County, Arizona. And my mother's full name was at long-last revealed to me.

Later, I would piece together that my loving Uncle Howard and Aunt Mildred had adopted me from Earl and my mother at my birth. "Howard Jordan"—as the return address stated—must have been Earl's brother. I never found out why I didn't see Uncle Howard and Aunt Mildred again, but at least they hadn't forgotten me. Somehow, they felt it was necessary to share the significant information of my birth with me. For that, and the joyful childhood memories they provided me, I will forever be grateful.

Jocinda

Jocinda's ears were now completely tuned into every word she heard.

Another way we are alike—I didn't know my mother.

Jocinda, too, had often thought about the woman who had given birth to her.

Does my mother have another family? Does she ever think of me or Violet? I don't remember ever celebrating Mother's Day. That used to make me sad, but after so many years, I've just stopped thinking about it. But maybe...

Jocinda wondered if she could look for her own mother when she got out of prison.

I wouldn't even know where to start. Does my birth certificate exist somewhere? There has to be records.

Maybe we could even be a family again.

The Search for My Mother

As I began the search for my mother, I didn't know where to begin. And yet, I couldn't deny the hope growing within me to fill this deep-seated longing to find her.

I examined what I now knew to be my birth certificate more closely, as if I were a detective looking for clues. I saw my mother's full name and that the document had been issued in Coconino County, whose county seat is Flagstaff, Arizona.

With excitement, I quickly picked up the phone and dialed 0 to get the telephone operator. When she answered, I told her I wanted to be connected with a woman in Flagstaff, Arizona, stating my mother's full name.

The operator replied, "Ma'am, I have lots of numbers for people with that name in Flagstaff."

My words gushing involuntarily, I told her how important it was for me to find this lady named Mary, explaining, "I just found my own birth certificate with this woman's name on it. Today is Mother's Day, and I just want to find her. She left me in the hospital 37 years ago, right after I was born."

The woman on the other end of the phone hesitated, then said, "I want to help. All I can do is give you the number for one person that matches that name." I jotted down the number and hung up.

With anticipation, I dialed the phone.

A young girl answered. I asked her if a woman named Mary lived there. The little girl quickly called out, "Grandma, someone wants to talk to you."

I waited just a brief moment. And then a sweet older voice said, "Hello."

I cheerfully replied, "Happy Mother's Day."

"Who are you?" the voice inquired.

"My name is Dana Louise Cryer," I responded. "Did you have a daughter thirty-seven years ago?" In the same breath, I told her my father's name.

She didn't respond.

I began rambling. "I'm 37 years old. I was born in Flagstaff. I have wanted to know my mother for so long. I was at church today, celebrating Mother's Day, when God told me to find the birth certificate I got in the mail several years ago. So I did. It is from Coconino County, and it has your name on it. So I called the operator and told them your name. She gave me this number. Somehow, I knew God wanted me to find you today. So I could wish you a happy Mother's Day. Are you my mother?"

I heard a sob on the other end of the line. And then the faint response, "You are my baby girl."

I instantly burst into tears. Mary was my mother, whom I had never seen but always yearned to meet one day. What an answer to prayer! It was a miracle that all this occurred as a result of the single prayer I had breathed that very morning at church. I could not believe the joy I felt. We both cried audibly, overcome with emotion. We couldn't even talk.

After a while, out of breath and full of emotions, we hung up, but not before I promised my mother that I would call her later.

I put the phone down in awe, astounded at all God had done for me in that single day. I prepared to return to evening service on that Mother's Day. This time, carrying the joy of having a mom of my own.

By the time I arrived at church, the reality of all that had occurred sunk in, and I began crying and shaking uncontrollably. I saw Brother Ferguson, and I told him I had a story. He didn't know the details, but He could tell by the joyful glow of my face that what had happened was an act of God. So when service began, he called me up to tell my story. When I did, the whole church broke into dancing and praise. I was bawling on the stage.

God! God! God!

It was all God who was able!

I had never been shy about telling my story, so everyone at church was aware of all I had gone through in my life. They also knew the yearning I had to find my mother. And now, God had made it possible in the most spectacular way. What a glorious Mother's Day celebration we had that year!

Jocinda

She found her! Maybe I can, too. Maybe that is why I am here today, listening to this lady. Maybe I am supposed to find my mother, too.

Jocinda's mind reeled. For the first time in years, she felt hope. It was something she was so unaccustomed to. It didn't feel right, but she allowed it in.

Maybe there is a woman still out there who wants to know her own "baby girls."

Jocinda felt a tear of sadness for all the years she had missed with her own mother, but her heart started to swell at the thought that maybe, just maybe, she and Violet were not really alone. She began to think of how she might start her search.

A small smile appeared on her face at the thought of something positive in her future.

Embracing My Mother

My mother and I proceeded to get acquainted through several phone conversations. I became so comfortable calling her "Mom," and she endearingly addressed me as "Hon."

Days after our initial conversation, I was at my desk at work when a co-worker brought me an envelope. Inside was a paid-for round-trip airplane ticket to Flagstaff, Arizona. "Someone heard of your miracle story and had me bring this to you. The person it is from does not want to be known, but they told me to tell you to please accept this blessing from God."

I was astounded. At long last, it was time. Not only had God given me the knowledge of who my mother was, but now He had provided the means for me to meet her face to face.

When I got home, I called Mary and excitedly told her, "Mom, I'm coming to meet you."

The next day, I arrived at work to a pile of money on my desk and a note that said, "We don't want you to travel alone. Please use this money to take someone with you."

I was overjoyed. I had wanted a traveling companion to make this very important trip with me, but I also knew our finances couldn't support it.

My husband Gene could not get away from work, and my older son Brent was committed to playing in a football game. So we decided that my younger son, Brad, who was then twelve years old, would accompany me.

Before I knew it, Brad and I were on an airplane, landing in Arizona.

When we arrived at Flagstaff Airport, I called a taxi to take my son and me to my mother's house. I anxiously got into the cab with butterflies fluttering about in my stomach. Becoming more nervous and excited about this meeting, I could hardly sit still in my seat. The driver sensed my anxiety and began making friendly conversation, "What brings you to Arizona?"

I briefly told him how I had found my mother on Mother's Day and that we were about to meet for the first time. "This trip is nothing short of a miracle."

I was caught off guard when our driver became very emotional. Composing himself, he asked if his wife, who worked for the local newspaper, could meet us to take some pictures so she could write and publish our story. I politely declined. I wanted to respect my mother and not embarrass or put her in an awkward position. I only wished to meet her.

We finally arrived. The driver smiled and announced, "We're here. You are about to meet your mama."

We pulled up to the house. I saw two women and a young girl on the front porch. Nervously, I fished in my purse and pulled out a camera my co-workers had given me. I handed the camera to my taxi driver, asking him if he would take pictures. Then, I reached for the door handle, peering out the window.

My heart beat faster as I saw my mother for the very first time. I could easily tell which woman she was when she stood up with tears rolling down her face.

I flung open the door as she descended the steps. Leaping out of the car, I couldn't run fast enough into her arms. We instantly embraced long and hard. She was much shorter than me. As I hugged her, I smelled her perfume. It was the same perfume I had worn for years. That similarity was just the first of many seeming coincidences we were to discover about each other.

Brad had made his way out of the car, followed by the taxi driver, who was snapping pictures. As I turned to look back, I noticed they were crying, too.

Mary finally caught her breath and, grabbing my hand, said, "Please come with me. I want you to meet my friends."

Walking toward the stairs, Mary introduced me to the other woman, Liz, and the teenage girl, Peggy, who I found out were mother and daughter.

Amid the commotion, the taxi driver excitedly guided us to pose for a picture so he could capture this meaningful moment. Afterward, he handed me the camera and hugged me, saying how amazing it was to share in our miracle story.

Jocinda

Well, isn't that just a Hallmark card? Not only does this woman find her mama, but someone gives her a plane ticket, a pile of money, AND a camera. That just doesn't happen.

Jocinda was drawing from a life of desperation. She had never been treated so nicely or been given things unexpectedly.

Then, even as she rolled her eyes, a strange new idea started to grow in her mind. It was like a baby plant coming through the dirt, searching for the sun.

Maybe, just maybe, this is all true. Maybe there is a God, and He does nice things for people.

The thought surprised Jocinda. It had been so long since she had a positive impression that it seemed almost foreign to her. She had been so lost in her own negative thoughts that this optimistic one was like a small voice speaking to her.

She wanted to hear more.

Getting to Know My Mother

Mary, Liz, and Peggy busied themselves preparing dinner. My mother knew nothing about me or my life. Nothing since the day I was born, that is. As we spoke, she hung on every detail I shared, and I relished being in her presence.

Through our conversation, I grew more and more amazed at how very much alike we were. Besides loving the same perfume, we shared similar clothing styles—for instance, we both loved bright colors. We also both belonged to Pentecostal churches and shared a love of being hospitable and preparing large amounts of food for others, always ready to have random people drop by.

As time passed, our conversation grew deeper, and we both began to open up more. Mary, who was full of questions and attentive to everything I said, put her work aside and sat down at the table with me. The heartfelt emotions emanating from her face made me realize she was incredibly empathetic.

For the first time, I began to realize that the pain from my story was not just mine. I was intricately connected to this woman who had been tortured for years by my absence from her life. The whole time that I had felt alone and abandoned, Mary was living her life while missing a part of her heart. In my grief, I had never paused long enough to think about how my story also affected others.

As our conversation unfolded, we began to trust each other more. Knowing that my mother deserved to hear the truth, I bared my tattered soul, sharing nearly everything—although I was not yet ready to disclose the sexual abuse that was such an integral part of my story. But I did tell how Earl had kidnapped me at the age of five and kept me in extreme isolation in a dirty, empty shack. And I described the mental, emotional, and physical abuse I had endured.

I paused as raw emotions overtook everyone in the room.

Mary and Liz both gasped as I recalled how I had sat in a jail cell staring at a picture of myself displayed on a missing child poster hanging on the wall.

"Why wouldn't anyone help you?" Mary wondered out loud. Then, with tears rolling down her cheeks, she grasped my hands, looked into my eyes, and asked, "Why didn't you speak up?"

They couldn't wrap their minds around the fact that I didn't understand what was happening to me.

Sighing deeply, I replied, "I've asked myself that a million times. I was missing, but somehow, I was invisible to the world. So I wasn't sure anyone would care."

Continuing, I told Mary and Liz how we had fled the state. "Much later, I realized Earl feared he would be in deep trouble if anyone figured out I was the missing girl on the poster."

I shared what it was like to live at Earl's house with the other children. Then, I guardedly explained the chain of events leading to Earl and Mara shooting each other. I still was not ready to unveil the details of what really caused them to assault each other so violently—my sexual abuse.

The room was quiet as I detailed being taken away from Earl's property and later learning that Earl was my biological father. My voice caught in my throat when I put into words how my heart shattered when the authorities separated me from my half-brothers. The air was still in the room as I chronicled my difficult years at the children's home and school. But then I finally shared how God had brought Gene and me together and given us our two beautiful sons.

I paused, reflecting in the silence that was cut only by my mother's weeping.

Mary wept in her friend's arms, saying how much she had suffered from the guilt and shame of abandoning me. "The last thing I knew about you was when I left you the day I walked away from the hospital." She felt at that moment that everything was her fault. The weight of the world was on her shoulders.

As my mother's shame and guilt pierced the air, the significant bond between the two friends before me became clear. Mary and Liz were deeply connected; they fully depended on each other.

I couldn't help but think how we all need others to help us get through the things we face. God had given me Gene and his family, my boys, and so many Christian sisters who came around me and became my support system. God never leaves us alone. As I saw my mother's pain unfold, I was so thankful for Liz and her daughter Peggy, who were obviously an ongoing support in her life.

Finally, realizing I was in a safe place with these women, I breathed deeply and mustered the strength to describe what had become the essence of my childhood: the raw, ongoing sexual abuse.

The sordid details were painful to speak out loud but were probably even more heart-wrenching for a mother to hear. We all thought it best that Peggy go into the other room for a bit so Mary could get herself together. I didn't know how old Peggy was, but she appeared to be a fragile pre-teen who surely wasn't ready to hear how cruel people can be.

Peggy obediently slipped away to the living room quietly. She was visibly disturbed, so it was good she was able to leave the room as I got deeper into the details of my abuse. We talked for hours; the two women and I huddled at the table, crying.

Over and over, her words barely understandable, Mary sobbed, "No, no, no. This can't be true. No one was there for you."

And over and over, I assured her I was now okay.

Through tears, she cried, "You endured so much trauma from your father forcing himself on you again and again. It's a miracle you are even alive and now have a family of your own. How were you able to come this far?"

I reflected knowingly, but continued on.

After many hours and emotions, Peggy returned and sat at the table, her own eyes wet with tears, as none of us could stop crying.

It wasn't until later that evening that I would find out the extent to which this had all affected sweet, young Peggy.

Brad, whom I had nearly forgotten about, came in from playing outside. We all decided to take a break and eat dinner. Afterwards, Mary got some towels for Brad and showed him where the shower was so he could get cleaned up after a long day of travel and playing outside. He soon fell soundly asleep.

The sun had long before gone down; Liz and Peggy announced it was time for them to return home as it was so late. After Mary and I walked them out, exhausted, we took baths and headed for bed.

Then, at 1:30 AM, I found myself being shaken awake by my mother. "Hon, wake up. I need you to come into the den."

Sleepily, I crawled out of bed and followed Mary, not knowing what to expect.

"Liz and Peggy are back. They just returned. They were pounding on the door, so I let them in, knowing something must be terribly wrong. I was right. We need you."

Jocinda

Jocinda wondered if her own mother might feel like Mary did.

Does she feel guilty for leaving me and Violet in such a horrible situation? Does she miss us? Does she want to find us? Could I ever have a tearful reunion with my own mother?

For a moment, Jocinda allowed her thoughts to dwell on the positive prospects of developing a relationship with her mother.

Then, just like a black cloud appearing out of nowhere, she had a different thought.

Maybe my mother is glad she left. Maybe she never wanted kids, and that's why she walked out.

Jocinda was sure her mother left because of the beatings she got, but could there be more? The smile that had begun to form on her face quickly disappeared, but Jocinda still had a small voice of hope inside. It would not be silenced. She was conflicted.

Hate and negative thinking have been part of who I am for as long as I can remember. What is this unfamiliar voice that will not let go?

Ripple Effects

I climbed out of bed, alert to my mother's plea, and followed her into the living room. Peggy and Liz were there. Following my mother's cues, I sat down on the couch as young Peggy crossed the room to sit next to me. She was trying to catch her breath from crying, burying her face in her hands.

"We have to talk to you," Liz began, her voice shaking with desperation. "As we left earlier tonight, Peggy said, 'Mom, the same thing that Ms. Dana said was happening to her with her dad has been happening to me. Daddy is having sex with me. All the time.'"

Liz burst into tears. She broke. Right in the living room.

Peggy continued crying with her face in her hands.

Liz was in shock. "This is the first time I have ever heard of this. I never suspected anything before, but maybe I was in denial."

I wrapped my arms around Peggy.

There was so much crying. The room was thick with emotion. Peggy had felt she could open up because I had shared my story. She reluctantly said that her daddy warned her that if she ever told anyone what he was doing to her, he would kill her.

I quickly thought back to the young girl's tears when she had returned from the other room earlier that evening. Apparently, the walls had not protected her from hearing my story, but maybe that was by God's design.

Breathlessly, Liz pleaded, "What would you do?"

Without hesitation, I told them to go straight to the police and tell them everything.

"I never had anyone to help me," I said as I remembered being in the jail cell and the police sending me back to Earl. "I had no voice. No one even let me speak or took notice of me. Even in the jail. I was completely filthy and neglected, wearing worn-out clothes that were far too small. I'm sure I stunk and looked emaciated. But they didn't care about me. They only cared that Earl was behind bars until he sobered up. And when he did, they let him out and released me back to him. Things would have been different if I had known to speak up."

"You have a voice, Peggy," I continued, "You need to go straight to the police. You are no longer in this alone. There are people who will help you, but first, you have to tell the police everything." Then I took her hands in mine and looked her in the eye. "Your daddy won't be able to do this to you anymore."

Both Peggy and Liz were still shaking, but they knew what they had to do. Now, with direction, they hugged us and left.

We looked out the window as they sat in the car for quite a while, composing themselves as they prepared to go to the police and stand against the evil that had been inflicted on them. Prepared or not, it was time to begin their healing journey.

I went back to bed, realizing that by bravely telling my story, by allowing other people into my dark secret, I had paved the way for another victim of the same kind of abuse to find a way out—a way out of the shame, guilt, and despair inflicted on her by no fault of her own.

We never know when God has someone who needs to hear our testimony. God had released me, and I knew He would release Peggy.

I have since had so many women tell me they are not strong enough to share what they have been through. They wonder how their story could help someone else.

I tell them to trust God. He alone is able to use even our worst circumstances for good, but we first have to let Him heal us and then tell people how He did it.

Other people have told me that they come from a Christian home with great parents, so they have no testimony. Wow! How blessed they are to be able to say that. But I say that everyone who walks with God has a story worth telling a hurting world.

No matter what your story is, if you let Him, God will use it to help someone else.

Telling my story gave Peggy the strength to tell hers and set her on a path of healing.

Jocinda

Strength. That is what it takes to tell that kind of story?

Jocinda knew she would never meet that little girl named Peggy, but she, Dana, and Jocinda all shared a bond. One that was built on something so terrible, so vile, so horrible. But one that created a link that could never be broken.

Jocinda started to cry for this little girl. She knew no one had ever cried for her and what she had endured, but now the tears streamed down her face in a mixture of white, hot rage for the man who had done this to a precious child and pity and love for the girl.

Jocinda knew she wanted to tell her own story someday.

She realized for the first time that giving voice to the terrible things that had happened in her life was the only way to get rid of the demons that haunted her.

This lady is right.

Jocinda could feel the gentle strength from Dana's story flowing into her.

A Hidden Wound

The next morning as we drank our coffee together, Mary told me she had not slept well because she was so distraught. She was having a difficult time dealing with knowing the truth of everything I had been through. I could tell that her lack of sleep now exacerbated her guilt and shame.

"I never told anyone," she began.

I remained quiet, not sure where she was going.

"I never told anyone how I left you. Nobody else knows how I abandoned you at the hospital. I kept it all a secret."

She paused as her pain filled the silence.

Taking a deep breath, she continued, "But I've thought about it a lot. To be honest, I've never stopped thinking about it. I never stopped thinking about you. You…the baby who had grown inside me. And I just left you. I walked out, not knowing who would take care of you. Who would feed you. Who would put your hair in pigtails. Who would tuck you into bed at night."

Tears rolled down Mary's face while I sat there processing my own emotions.

"I always imagined you out there somewhere. The thoughts suffocated me. Like somebody putting a pillow over my face. I couldn't breathe. It hurt so bad. But inside, I knew I deserved the pain. I deserved all that shame and guilt that never left me. Sometimes I thought about ending it all, thinking about how selfish I was. I left you alone at the hospital with that monster. I can never forgive myself. I ruined your life, and I ruined mine."

Stunned at her outpouring, my brain swirled. I realized that deep within me, I still harbored agonizing pain that stemmed from my mother's choice to leave me.

I thought I had come so far. I had, after all, forgiven the man who had tormented me physically for so many years. But now I understood I still carried emotional turmoil from being abandoned by the woman who had given birth to me.

I paused as I felt a torrent of tears fall down my face, washing the hurt and anger from my soul. As I listened to my mother's heartfelt words, I could empathize with her pain. And with God's help, I released my own pain. By walking out on me, my mother had stabbed me, causing excruciating wounds that would fester and become infected over so many years. Now, I finally allowed God to soften those barbed edges of my tattered soul. Though I wasn't immediately healed, at the very moment I saw my mother's lament, the infection was irrigated, and my heart was bandaged and prepared to heal as the piercing pain began to subside within me.

I carefully considered my response, knowing I finally had the power to forgive her.

"We've both been through so much—more than anyone should have to endure. God is allowing me to see the pain you must have carried all these years. But He is so good, and if you let Him help you and learn to forgive yourself as I forgive you, I know He will help you get beyond those crippling thoughts. I know, because I have been where you are."

My mother looked at me with sorrow. With strength and compassion, I put my hand on hers, looked her straight in the eyes, and continued.

"For so many years, hate, anger, and bitterness took over my life. I now understand that my pain came not only from all Earl took from me but also from the grief of you abandoning me. I felt so unwanted. I didn't even know what love was."

My mother tried to pull away. I knew I had hurt her, but she needed to understand my pain so she could truly heal.

"I also came to a point when I didn't want to live anymore. I even planned to kill myself. But at the last minute, I didn't do it."

She refocused on me, asking, "Why? What stopped you?"

I paused as I realized God was giving me an amazing opportunity to share the most important truth ever. I weighed every word, understanding their importance.

I described my intention of committing suicide and how the angel had visited me, touching my shoulder. I shared in detail about the moment Jesus entered my heart as I fell on the bed and prayed to Him. Only He was able. It was God who was able to release all my hate, anger, and bitterness. He took away my grief of abandonment and the pain Earl had inflicted; only God allowed me to forgive my tormentor. I told her I could never have done any of this on my own. It was only in my submission to Jesus, my Savior, and accepting His forgiveness that I was given the power to forgive others.

My mother listened to all I had to say in silence. We talked about Jesus a little more, and then we prayed together. I knew God would continue to work in her heart as He had worked in mine.

The time arrived for Brad and me to leave. My mother and I said our goodbyes, vowing to see each other again.

I returned home, grateful to have finally met my mom and spend those few priceless days with her. I was even more awed that God had released in me a pain that had been buried so deeply I didn't even know it existed. God carefully and expertly brought my wounds from being abandoned by my mother to the surface of my heart and then carefully stitched up the lacerations with His threads of compassion and restoration, allowing me to breathe more deeply and freely than I ever had.

But my heart still grieved because my mother, who I now loved deeply, was carrying such a heaviness and was still so full of unforgiveness toward herself.

When I got home, I unloaded everything that happened to Gene. It was such an emotional time. He told me, "You're not done there. You have to go back. There is more. You're not done yet with your mom."

Days passed. Mary and I communicated with each other over the phone. I continued to share Jesus' message of salvation and tell her again and again I fully forgave her; reminding her that my forgiveness was possible only because I knew how completely Jesus had forgiven me.

I didn't let too much time pass before I scheduled another trip to see her. I knew Gene was right—I needed to see my mother in person again. The next time I traveled, I went alone.

When I arrived, she greeted me with the biggest smile on her face. We were both so excited to talk in person again. But there was more.

With excitement, Mary said she had something big to tell me.

Her words came pouring out like a full-on waterfall.

"I finally get it! I finally took to heart everything you said about forgiveness. Now I am free! It's been 72 years that I've been in an emotional prison, but now I am free."

Jocinda

*F*orgiveness.

That word keeps coming up.

First, the lady forgave her daddy, who made her life a living hell. And now her mama was forgiving herself for walking out on her baby and letting her grow up in such an awful situation.

As Jocinda sat there, she wondered if she could ever forgive her parents. She harbored hate for her daddy for all the years of abuse and neglect. She couldn't understand how her own mama could just leave her and Violet. She even hated herself for not doing something sooner to help herself and Violet.

I don't think I can ever forgive like these people did.

Then she remembered the part of the lady's story about strength. She had said that her testimony had given the little girl the strength to tell her own story about how her daddy had abused her.

Do I have the strength within me to forgive?

For the first time in her life, Jocinda considered that she just might.

Freedom for Mary

Mary continued detailing how God had been working in her life since we had last seen each other.

"I wept uncontrollably every time I thought of you," she told me. "I couldn't understand how you had forgiven me. Hearing about all you went through as a child, all that I could have prevented if I had never left you, filled me with so much shame. It actually made me sick to my stomach. I couldn't eat. I couldn't sleep. It got to the point where I couldn't think of anything else."

"My pain got so deep that, one day, I purposely stepped in front of a car speeding down the road. It was the only way I could think to stop the agonizing pressure of thoughts chasing me. I wanted to end my life. Miraculously, the car that should have killed me swerved sharply, missing me by just inches."

I grabbed her warm hand, not believing what I was hearing. Thankful for God's mercy on her life.

She went on, "I fell to the ground and looked up to God through my tears, seeing His hand at work protecting me."

I smiled. She had seen that it was God, too.

"I should have been dead." Silence filled the air. And then she smiled so brightly. "But I am ALIVE!"

"After He kept me from dying," Mary continued, "I immediately felt an overwhelming need to talk to my pastor. So I hurried over to my church. When the pastor came out, I broke down, admitting to the hidden shame and guilt that had held me captive for so many years. I confessed to him that my pain had gotten so bad that I saw no way out other than ending my life. But praise God! He had intervened!"

As this precious woman and I sat outside on the lawn, we both looked up at the beautiful clouds overhead. I was pausing and thanking God for His overwhelming goodness. Little did I know, the best part of the story was yet to come.

My birth mother, whom I had longed to know for a lifetime, was about to share with me the most heartwarming news that she and I would never be separated again—God had made a way for our spirits to unite for eternity.

Mary revealed that on that day, which had begun as awful but would soon become the best day of her life, her pastor spoke to her about forgiveness. He told her how we are able to forgive ourselves and others because Jesus made a way by forgiving us.

"So I sat there with the pastor, and I asked for Jesus' forgiveness—which had been there all along. What I really needed to do was accept His forgiveness and allow Him to release me of all the shame and guilt I had held since that day I gave birth to you and refused to hold you in my arms or even look in your eyes."

"Last time we met, you gifted me, Dana, by giving me your forgiveness. Your example showed me what true forgiveness looks like. And although I can't truly understand how grace works, I know that our God is able to overcome any wrong we have done in our lives—even my wrongs that hurt you so badly. God's forgiveness and mercy are unending. Sitting there with the pastor, I finally knew for certain that God had always been with me, ready to shower me with His incredible love. I just had to accept it."

My mother took a deep breath as I looked into her eyes.

"And I did, my baby girl. I accepted God's love. And He saved me. And now, despite what I have done, I get to spend eternity with Him. And because you are His too, I get to spend forever with you."

We celebrated and hugged, thanking God for all He had done in both our lives. Our God. He who is able!

Jocinda

J ocinda began to see the pieces of the puzzle coming together.

This lady who came to speak to all the inmates is here to reach ME.

Jocinda didn't know how she knew this, but she did. She felt a connection with this lady unlike anyone she had ever known, and yet they had not even spoken a word directly to each other.

Their stories were so similar. But their lives were so different.

What gave this lady the strength to walk out of such a hellish place and be ok? She keeps talking about God. I don't know much about God, but I know going through life requires strength. I had the strength to survive, but there's a voice in me that keeps asking if I have the strength to really live.

I keep listening to the lady, but I keep hearing that other voice inside me, like a friend who knows me. It's making me think about these things...making me feel things that I haven't in years...maybe ever. But I do now.

I wonder if the woman speaking to this group...speaking directly to ME...has her own small voice.

I bet she does.

Going Home

My trip ended so beautifully, providing me the closure I needed to fly home. I knew God had allowed this time to birth a true ministry in my life that would involve sharing the miraculous way He had reached me and my family with His love.

Mary and I talked about what was to come next. We were both anticipating the future that God had in store for us as mother and daughter. We looked forward to more visits, talking and laughing on the phone, and the wonder of sharing Mother's Day together.

Mary had told me about her other children, my half-siblings, David and Esther. I was excited to meet them in person, but I wasn't sure when that would happen. David and I began a relationship through phone conversations, and we eventually met. He was a handsome Christian man. Unfortunately, Esther and I never met.

Returning home from that visit with my mother, I felt as if a weight I didn't even know I had been carrying was lifted off my shoulders. Suddenly, I not only had a mother here on earth, but I had a mother who was saved by the grace of God and would be with me for eternity. The lightness and joy I felt was evident as I shared with Gene and my sons how Mary had experienced the saving grace of Jesus. Brent and Brad smiled knowingly. It was then I realized they knew exactly how I felt. As children, they had prayed for my salvation and were thrilled when I had come to know Jesus. Now, they saw me and my prayers being answered for my own mother's salvation.

Unfortunately, my season of knowing my mother on earth was short-lived. Soon after arriving home, my half-brother David called to share that my mother had been taken to the hospital. He told me she was very sick with complications from her diabetes. I felt the urge to fly out to see her again immediately. As I was preparing to go, however, I got another call that my birth mother had died. The woman I had just reconnected with had been taken home to be with Jesus.

Although my heart was broken, I was overcome with an undeniable peace that only God was able to give me. I was so grateful for the opportunity to meet my mother, offer her my own forgiveness, and then see her set free through the grace God had been waiting to lavish upon her. And now, in His perfect timing, he took her home to live in peace and joy with Him forever.

I was comforted beyond all understanding, knowing I would see my mother again in heaven.

Dana

Standing in front of the prisoners, Dana reached for a tissue and wiped her tears. The room was silent.

My time is almost over, but I need to share with these ladies that God's hope is for them, just as it was for me and my family. I have to tell them that God is the source of our hope. He enables us to go on despite anything the world throws at us.

I know there are women in this audience yearning for a reason to go on. God, give me the words to reach them.

A God Who Is Able

I've told this story so many times, and people always ask me, "Dana, how did you do it? How did you get beyond all you went through? How did you forgive, Dana? How? How? How?"

There's no denying that from the first moments of my life on earth, I was abandoned. I lived in such darkness for years and years. The confusion and fear I felt from the day I was taken turned quickly to serious pain, then loneliness, and eventually to anger. It took me a long time to recognize that darkness had taken over my soul, making me feel unworthy of being loved or even living.

I only became as strong as I did because God told me that one day, I would minister to hurting people with my story. Through helping others, He has brought me deliverance. I grew up not speaking to anyone, unable to communicate or even acknowledge my thoughts and feelings. But our amazing God has guided and directed me. And now, He has gifted me with the ability to speak so that I am able to do exactly what He has asked me to do.

But my journey did not begin with speaking or telling my story at all. God met me in the darkness, pulling me to His side.

He surrounded me with His love in so many ways. He sent angels and people and situations to show me His heart for me. God was so patient as He gently prodded me into understanding Him more.

Our faithful Father encompassed me fully, teaching me to pray and allowing me to understand scripture despite never having had the proper schooling and barely being able to read or write. He showed me that He will always be there to help me with all the puzzles of life as I follow Him. And He will be there for you, too, if you let Him.

Now, I love my life because I get to share it. What the enemy meant for evil, God turned around for His good. Many years ago, I heard God say to me, "Dana, you are going to use your story for My glory." Now, through His power and strength, I am able to do just that.

Through His grace, I have come to recognize that despite all I endured, I wasn't the only one in pain.

My daddy, Earl, living in a completely different kind of pain, spent most of his life in a dark pit of addiction and selfish rage. He was trapped, continually making wrong decision after wrong decision—for reasons he probably didn't even clearly understand.

My mother, Mary, was ongoingly tormented by the agony of deserting her own child. She lived in constant worry about what had become of me. Despair enveloped her, causing tremendous grief and making her hide behind her shame and guilt. For so many years, she wasn't able to live her life freely. She struggled to tell the truth, determined to hide her past and all she had done—labeling herself unforgivable.

Perhaps as you've heard my life story, you've related to one of these hurting people. No matter where you are—if you have been abandoned; if you have been hurt, abused, or molested by someone else and have lashed out in response; if you have been burdened by the shackles of addiction; or if you carry the guilt of a wrong choice and feel you cannot be forgiven—I'm here to tell you that God loves you and has a heart to embrace you where you are.

This story isn't about me right now. This is about you and what God is doing in your heart as you hear it. Every single one of us has pain that we think no one else can understand. We all have times when we walk through unfathomable darkness. Grim times that seem unbearable.

But through it all, God's light can permeate every bleak situation. Only God is good. And He calls us into His presence and gives us His power to stand strong no matter what comes against us. When negative or harmful thoughts invade your spirit, God is able to release you. Cry out to Him.

This is the whole point of my message to you today: You can trust God.

You are precious in His sight. God alone is able to fill your life with peace. He is able to heal and comfort you. And only God is able to give you eternity through salvation and His Son.

Wherever you are and whatever you've been through, Jesus is waiting for you. By offering yourself to Him—by releasing your pain, sorrow, wrongdoings, mistakes, guilt, hopes, and joys—He will adopt you into His family through His love and forgiveness.

There is nothing so bad that God can't forgive. Whatever you've done, if you go to Him, He will hear you.

The Bible tells us that *If we tell Him our sins, He is faithful and we can depend on Him to forgive us of our sins. He will make our lives clean from all sin* (1 John 1:9 NLV).

God's forgiveness will usher in a special kind of love that can give you a new perspective.

Right now, you may be thinking of someone who has hurt you, knowing with your whole being that you could never forgive that person for whatever he or she has done to you. You aren't wrong to feel hurt and betrayed.

But when you allow God's love and grace to enter your life, you will also gain His perspective, which will permeate your life and miraculously allow you to forgive others.

I know. You've heard how I have been there. I was hurt. I was angry. I was bitter. I was resentful. But when I went to God, seeking His forgiveness for all I had become, He allowed me to forgive others for their unimaginable offenses.

When you cry to God and ask Him for His forgiveness, He will give you so much more. God is waiting to pardon you. He is longing to cleanse you and make you as white as snow so He can show others His love through you. He has promised us all this in His Word, saying, *Blessed are those whose transgressions are forgiven, whose sins are covered. Blessed is the one whose sin the Lord will never count against them* (Romans 4:7-8 NIV).

If you are feeling imprisoned by hate and rage as I was, please open your heart to God. You can begin simply by reading scripture. God will unleash His power to cleanse and heal you as you read the Bible. Step into His presence, and He will flood your soul with a strength and resolve to guide you toward the holiness He has created for you to walk in. God assures us, *Whether you turn to the right or to the left, your ears will hear a voice behind you, saying, "This is the way; walk in it"* (Isaiah 30:21 NIV).

By His grace, I can share what only God was able to do. After I accepted His forgiveness, God's love infused in me a longing for my mother and daddy's salvation. I knew they both needed Him as much as I did. I was able to offer my forgiveness to them as a glimpse of everything He had waiting for them. Offering them my forgiveness through His power brought me release, knowing that through it, God was preparing them for His freedom.

I look forward to seeing my birth parents in heaven. We each individually came to Him requesting His grace and mercy, and our God, who alone is able, was exuberant to grant us eternity with Him. I know my parents are now perfected in His glory—because that's what God promises to do for us. It is with joy I can say all three of us will be with Jesus together forever. And He is waiting to do the same for you.

Without God, we are nothing. No matter your credentials, what fancy shoes you wear, or where you lay your head at night, you are no one without inviting Jesus in your heart.

You can trust Jesus with your life. God promises that His plan for you is beyond what you could ask or imagine. He tells us, *I will go before you and will level the mountains; I will break down gates of bronze and cut through bars of iron. I will give you hidden treasures, riches stored in secret places, so that you may know that I am the Lord, the God of Israel, who summons you by name* (Isaiah 45:2-3 NIV).

You have a decision to make. You've heard my whole story. I am who I am only because of God's ever-present love for me.

And His love will allow you to be who He designed you to be, too. Despite the dank walls surrounding you here in this prison or wherever you go in the world, God's brightness can enfold your heart for eternity, wiping clean your past and giving you the peace and assurance that you belong to Him.

Are you willing to accept God and His love? Are you willing to let Him in? Are you willing to try to understand what He is saying to you right now? They are the same words He said to me when I was at my lowest and couldn't even begin to understand...

JESUS LOVES YOU!

You can trust God. You can trust Him with your darkest thoughts and most painful memories. You can trust Him with your fears, your insufficiencies, and your pain. God alone is able to overcome anything in your life. He is that powerful! Believe me. I know!

Will you let Him in? Will you tell Him that you are ready to try? Will you tell Him that you want to release everything you have carried for years and years? Maybe even for your entire life?

God is calling you to open your heart. Some of you may be feeling the excitement of this moment. If you are, I want to pray with you. But if you are still processing everything I've been saying, I want to encourage you to keep listening, not to me, but to that still, small voice in your head and heart. That is God reaching out to you.

God is patient, and His timing is perfect. He will never give up on you. Just like He never gave up on me.

His love for you for you is outshining any darkness that may have come upon you in your life.

Know that God understands what you are thinking right now, and He wants to hear from your heart. What you say matters to Him. He sees you. He hears you. And He knows you better than you know yourself.

Will you invite Jesus to come into your heart to be your Lord and Savior? If so, pray this prayer in your heart as I pray it out loud.

Dear Father God,

I come to You with an open heart. I ask You to make a change in me this very minute. You've come to set me free. Thank You, Holy Spirit, for touching me right now. You are here to alleviate my pain, heal my hurtful memories, and put me on Your path.

I can't even comprehend that Your infinite love is enveloping me right now as I cry out to You. You are holding me in Your hand. Nothing is impossible for You.

I am sorry for all I've done that has hurt You. I choose to allow You to come into my life and be Lord over all I do. Thank You for forgiving me and healing my brokenness. Please help me forgive those who have hurt me.

Jesus, I invite You to come into my heart and be my savior.

Father, Son, and Holy Spirit, I praise You. I lift my hands to heaven and proclaim, only YOU ARE ABLE. You are my maker, provider, and savior. You are my everything.

I praise You for Your goodness that brings me freedom. I trust You to guide me from this day forward.

I pray this in Jesus' name.

Amen.

God's Plan Fulfilled

Tears streamed down my face as I stepped from the stage, flanked by the attendants prepared to usher me out.

Just then, I heard the cries of an inmate pleading with the guards to allow her to speak with me. I looked over and instantly recognized the woman from the second row with whom my eyes had connected during my first moments on stage. Initially, she had exhibited an angry demeanor clothed in apathy. But as I told my story, her composure softened. At times, she even looked interested as a glow of hope seemed to overcome her.

Pulled, I veered in her direction and was soon standing in front of her.

"My name is Jocinda," she said. "What happened to you happened to me, too. But you're there, and I'm here. I killed my daddy after what he did to me. That's why I'm in here. I know you said a lot about God and strength and forgiveness, but I don't know about all that. I don't know if I could ever forgive him for what he did to me. And I know he can't forgive me because he is dead."

I paused for a moment and looked into this woman's eyes. I felt her hurt, humiliation, betrayal, and fear. This poor lady had walked the same road I had, but we had ended up at different places. I prayed in my heart for God to give me the words to help her understand that only through His strength and His compassion could she ever be able to extend forgiveness. I reached out and held her hand, feeling the years of pain bottled up inside of her.

She continued, "But that voice you talked about. I hear it. It just won't go away. I was beginning to think I was crazy. It keeps asking me questions I don't know the answer to, and every time you talk about God, it's like it's telling me to listen."

"Honey, that's the Holy Spirit. God is talking to you. He wants you to know you are loved. He needs you to know that He forgives you, and if He is willing to do that, you can forgive anyone and have the strength to do anything."

Jocinda was clearly worn and tired from what life had done to her, and she was longing for something more. I knew our time together was brief and that she was suddenly opening up to me in a way that was surely unusual for her. I didn't want to rush her. But when God gives us an assignment, we can be assured that He will accomplish His will through us if we trust His timing and respond in obedience.

Following the Holy Spirit, I went right to the point and asked her if she knew Jesus.

"I know a little about Him, but I don't know Him. I've never heard anyone say He loves me, like you did."

I felt the attendant touch my arm, trying to hurry me out of the room. But I resisted, knowing there was something far more important at stake.

I focused in on Jocinda as our eyes locked and said with all the clarity I could muster: "Jesus loves you. And He wants to comfort you and bring peace to your troubled heart."

Then, I asked her if we could pray together. She said she didn't know how to do that.

"All you have to do is say what's on your heart—or even think the words. Jesus loves you and will hear you."

She smiled and said ok.

We both bowed our heads, and I asked our heavenly Father to give my new friend Jocinda peace and allow her to feel His love. I thanked the Holy Spirit for speaking to her and asked Him to continue moving within her heart. I prayed that God would heal her relationships, show her how to forgive those who had hurt her, and give her the strength to overcome what she couldn't do in her own power.

As I prayed, Jocinda's hand was trembling. I felt her pain and wanted her to know the joy and peace that can only be found in a relationship with Jesus.

After, she looked up at me and said softly, "Thank you for praying for me. I don't understand it all, but it feels right."

We both smiled as the guards led her away with the other inmates.

I will never know for certain until I get to heaven, but I believe God brought me to that prison on that day for Jocinda. She understood the pain and hurt I had endured, and I could see the love she needed in her life.

She needed my God. The God Who Is Able.

Afterword

Since accepting Jesus into my life, it has been my joy and honor to continue serving Him with everything in me.

Gene and I are still together and in love to this very day. Besides our two sons, Brent and Brad, God has now blessed us with our daughters-in-love, Kim Cryer and Katie Cryer, and three grandsons, Cade, Jace, and Nick. We continue to love and serve Jesus in our community of Pottsboro, Texas, and around the world as God leads us, witnessing many salvations and healings as God has used my life story to testify of His amazing grace.

As I tell this story today, I feel so blessed because we do not know how our lives can touch someone else. I know that I have a sacred walk with Jesus. It is hard to put into words, but to know Jesus the way I do is so wonderful. God never left me alone, even when I didn't see it. I love my Jesus with all my heart, and I thank Him that I can now be an extension of His love by sharing how He taught me to forgive.

It makes me think of the Bible verse Ephesians 6:12, which says, *Our fight is not against human beings. It is against the rulers, the authorities and the powers of this dark world. It is against the spiritual forces of evil in the heavenly world* (NIRV).

I have often recalled how, as a child, my mind couldn't comprehend everything happening to me. The years of abuse I endured caused me to feel dirty, scared, and fearful of what other people thought of me or might do to me. But God reassured me, saying, "When your father and mother abandoned you, I took you in."

God our Father did more than take me in under His wing: He provided me with complete and true healing. And He will do the same for you, too.

Jesus died for all our sins. He died because He and His Father God did not want any one of His children to suffer for eternity in hell. He died so we could receive complete forgiveness and learn to offer that same forgiveness to others. God knew from the beginning of time what was in front of us and what we would endure.

As I was flying on the plane from Texas to Florida to meet Kimberly Hobbs and Julie Jenkins to begin the mission of writing this book, I asked God if I was doing the right thing by sharing everything openly with the world. He said, "Yes. I wrote your story before you were born. I have called you by name and picked who would read your story for such a time as this. I knew your father and mother would abandon you—it was not because I didn't love you, but because they did not know Me. I had a plan that you would surrender to Me and open your life so others could see how much I love them, too."

Oh, how blessed I've been throughout my life!

God wants to bless you, too! He wants you to relax in His everlasting arms. The eternal God is your refuge. When you are weak, He is strong. He wants to carry you.

God is saying to you today, "Rest in Me! Refresh yourself in My presence!"

He has given you the freedom to release your cares and worries and receive His peace. Open your heart and mind to grasp all He has for you. God wants you to talk to Him about your struggles, fears, and broken relationships. Just be honest about how you are feeling and ask for His wisdom.

If any of you lacks wisdom, you should ask God, who gives generously to all without finding fault, and it will be given to you (James 1:5 NIV).

The Good Shepherd stands ready to lead you and anoint you with His healing, soothing oil of gladness!

You can trust God! He wants to shine His light into your heart! There's absolutely no love greater than Jesus' love!

Thank you for reading my book. I pray your life has been impacted for eternity by the truth of Jesus—the One who loves you and *Who Is Able* to set you free.

ABOUT THE AUTHORS

God brought together Kimberly Ann Hobbs and Julie T. Jenkins to chronicle the story of Dana Louise Cryer in *Who Is Able?* Kimberly and Julie serve as co-CEOs of World Publishing and Productions, whose mission is to guide and assist writers and artists to share their God-given stories with the world. They have helped hundreds of authors grow in their giftings and present their completed works to the world. Kimberly and Julie also serve as co-CEOs of Women World Leaders, a ministry that seeks to empower women to fulfill their God-given purpose as leaders for Christ. Together, they lead an amazing team of women as they broadcast a weekly podcast, publish a quarterly magazine called *Voice of Truth*, and present leadership training opportunities.

Kimberly is also a best-selling author (*Tears to Triumph, Courageous Steps of Faith, Surrendered, Embrace the Journey, Victories, Hope Alive*), an artist, sits on the Kerus Global Education advisory board, and supports her husband Ken in his ministry, United Men of Honor. Together, Ken and Kimberly serve in missions and ministry and run their own financial coaching company. They have children and grandchildren whom they love very much.

Michael Jenkins, Julie's husband of nearly 30 years, joined the WPP team to write Jocinda's story. Michael is a devout Christian who serves as a senior vice president of Hope Media Group and WayFM, a national contemporary Christian music and media ministry. He is a regional Emmy recipient and a seven-time Ad Federation award winner for his work in television production and sales. Additionally, Michael is a contributing author to WPP's best-selling book, *Navigating Your Storm*.

Julie's passion is editing. She is also a best-selling author (*Courageous Steps of Faith, Surrendered, Embrace the Journey, Victories, Miracle Mindset*), earned a Bachelor of Communications from The University of Tulsa and a Masters of Biblical Exposition from Moody Bible College, traveled with Up With People, was a long-time Bible Study Fellowship leader and teacher, and has completed multiple biblical and leadership training programs. Julie and Michael have three children, of whom they are immensely proud.

MORE FROM WPP

World Publishing and Productions was birthed in obedience to God's call. Our mission is to empower writers to walk in their God-given purpose as they share their God story with the world. We offer one-on-one coaching and a complete publishing experience. To find out more about how we can help you become a published author or to purchase books written to share God's glory, please visit: worldpublishingandproductions.com

God longs for you to have ferocious faith grounded in His unwavering love. *Unshakable: God Will Sustain You* will propel you on a transformative journey as you witness God's sustaining power. Every trial and triumph of this shaky world can become an opportunity to harness and deepen your faith in God.

The authors of *Unseen: You Are Not Alone* share their struggles of feeling isolated and unnoticed and detail how our awesome God helped them overcome every obstacle to find what truly matters: Him. These stories and devotional teachings shed light on the truth of your significance and value. You are never alone!

Despite all the adversities we face, God is the source of our hope. In this book, you will see firsthand how God brings *Hope Alive* to every person who is yearning for a reason to go on. Like a broken tree in a dark place is primed for new growth, God can use the rich soil of your dark place to prepare a new life to sprout in you.

Life is full of storms and rough waters. The stories and teachings in *Navigating Your Storm: By United Men of Honor* will give you the ability to see the light of God and navigate your storm victoriously, no matter how strong the waves coming against you may seem.

The authors of *Miracle Mindset: Finding Hope in the Chaos*, have experienced the wonders of God's provision, protection, and guidance. These stories and teachings will ignite a spark within you, propelling you to encounter the marvel of God's miracles, even in the chaos.

By harnessing God's power of *Joy Unspeakable: Regardless of Your Circumstances*, you will learn how joy and sorrow can dance together during adversity. The true stories and insightful teachings in this book will encourage, inspire, motivate, and give you hope, joy, and peace.

United Men of Honor: Overcoming Adversity Through Faith will help you armor up, become fit to fight, and move forward with what it takes to be an honorable leader. Over twenty authors in this book share their accounts of God's provision, care, and power as they proclaim His Word.

Victories: Claiming Freedom in Christ presents expository teaching coupled with individual stories that testify to battles conquered victoriously through the power of Jesus Christ. The words in this book will motivate and inspire you and give you hope as God awakens you to your victory!

Embrace the Journey: Your Path to Spiritual Growth will strengthen and empower you to step boldly in faith. These stories, along with expertly placed expositional teachings will remind you that no matter what we encounter, we can always look to God, trusting HIS provision, strength, and direction.

Surrendered: Yielded With Purpose will help you recognize with awe that surrendering to God is far more effective than striving alone. When we let go of our own attempts to earn God's favor and rely on Jesus Christ, we receive a deeper intimacy with Him and a greater power to serve Him.

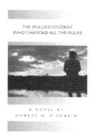
Riley Rossey is not your everyday bullied student, but one who discovers how to use his talents to assist other shy and picked-on individuals. Journey with Riley as he meets bullying head-on and becomes a God-given blessing to so many in *The Bullied Student Who Changed All the Rules* by Robert M. Fishbein.

At seventeen, Audrey Marie experienced a sudden and relentless excruciating firestorm of pain. *Chronically Unstoppable* tells of her true-life journey as she faced pain, developed strength, and battled forward with hope.

Heartbeat of a Survivor tells the story of Nita Tin, a Buddhist born and raised in an opulent lifestyle in Burma. As her country came under the control of a ruthless military dictator, Nita's whole life changed. Forced to flee her home, her soul was soon set free in a greater way than she ever dreamed possible.

The world has become a place where we don't have a millisecond to think, often leaving us feeling lost or overwhelmed. That is why Max Gold wrote *Planestorming!*—a straightforward guide to help you evaluate and change your life. It's time to get to work and make the rest of your life the BEST of your life.